China, 1860

General Sir Hope Grant, by Beato, 1860
(courtesy of the Director, National Army Museum)

China, 1860

MICHAEL MANN

MICHAEL RUSSELL

© Michael Mann 1989

First published in Great Britain 1989
by Michael Russell (Publishing) Ltd
The Chantry, Wilton, Salisbury, Wiltshire

Typeset at The Spartan Press Ltd
Lymington, Hampshire
Printed and bound in Great Britain
by Biddles Ltd, Guildford and King's Lynn

Contents

Glossary

abattis: a defence normally formed by placing trees or bamboo lengthwise one over the other, with their branches towards the enemy.

daffadar: Indian Army term for a sergeant of cavalry.

gingal: a heavy type of musket, used in China and India.

joss-house: a Chinese temple.

kot-daffadar: Indian Army term for troop sergeant-major of cavalry.

li: a Chinese measurement of distance of just under half a mile.

sowar: Indian Army term for a trooper of cavalry.

tope: Indian term for a clump of trees.

wan: Chinese for a bay.

yamun: a Chinese official residence or office, often the house of a mandarin.

I

British interest in China in the early nineteenth century rested primarily upon trade. For many years both the French and the British had wanted to open up commerce with the lucrative Chinese market, and this began for the British with the exchange of cloth and cotton from India in return for tea and silk. But it was opium that soon dominated the scene, with the East India Company growing large stocks which it shipped to China, where demand was insatiable. The Indian Government taxed this trade and became heavily dependent upon its revenue. Whereas silver had to be paid to the Chinese to cover the value of the silk and tea imports while cotton remained the principal British export from India, with the rapid growth of the opium trade this balance was reversed and China had to pay silver to India.

The Imperial Chinese Government treated all foreigners with profound contempt and suspicion, continually placing severe restrictions on their ability to trade and on their freedom of movement. Furthermore the Imperial Chinese Government was anxious to stop the opium trade which was having such a disastrous effect upon its people. 'Free trade' may have seemed an honourable objective to the European conscience, but that trade consisted in great part of an opium traffic which undermined the health of the Chinese people – albeit providing an extremely lucrative commerce to the traders involved, and essential revenue to the Government of India. Chinese attempts to control this trade led to the First China War of 1839–42.

From the British point of view the war was fought in order to secure satisfactory trading facilities. These were established by the Treaty of Nanking, signed in 1842, which opened the ports of Canton and Shanghai to European trade, though relationships between the British and Chinese authorities were seldom satisfactory. In 1856 a second conflict began because the Chinese were refusing to honour the Treaty obligations. They had, in addition, both executed a French missionary and stopped a British ship, from which they removed twelve Chinese sailors who were accused of piracy and summarily executed. On the one side was the general European dissatisfaction with the restrictions placed upon foreign trade in China, and the contemptuous Chinese attitude to all 'foreign barbarians'; on the other was the Chinese sense of cultural superiority, and suspicion of Western intentions.

The Treaty of Tientsin was agreed in June 1858, at the end of the Second China War, when Britain and France brought pressure to bear upon the Chinese to allow a Resident Minister from each country to be maintained in China. In the following year Admiral Hope was sent with a fleet of nineteen British vessels to escort the two Resident Ministers to their new posts. This fleet gathered in the Gulf of Pechilli, where it was joined by Mr Bruce, the British Resident, and M. de Bourboulon, the French Minister-Designate. Admiral Hope sailed ahead of the main fleet and arrived at the mouth of the Pei-ho river, leading to Peking, where he anchored off Taku on 17 June 1859. However, when he sent an envoy ashore to negotiate the arrival of the two Resident Ministers, he was met on the beach by a crowd of undisciplined armed Chinese, who refused to permit anyone to land and told the envoy that if any attempt should be made to enter the Pei-ho river, it would be resisted. The river itself, they said, was blocked by underwater obstructions.

The two Resident Ministers joined Hope on 20 June, but left it to him to take any initiative in opening up the river. After several days of argument with the Chinese, the Admiral decided to attack the Taku forts that guarded the entrance to the Pei-ho. On 25 June a force of gunboats opened fire on these forts, and at the same time a party of 1,100 Royal Marines and sailors landed to storm them. The Chinese at Taku were commanded by General Sankolinsin, and as their gunners opened a heavy and accurate fire, they managed to sink or disable four British gunboats. The Marines and sailors of the landing party, wading ashore, were pinned down on the muddy flats by the ferocity of the barrage. Admiral Hope was badly wounded in the gunboat in which he had hoisted his flag, and only nine of the sailors in his boat were left standing and fit for action. As Hope was transferred to another vessel, he was wounded a second time. He would hardly have escaped had not Commodore Tatnall of the United States Navy, who was standing off with a number of American ships, ordered those under his command to tow in the British reserves. These had been left standing out to sea and had no other means of coming to the aid of their compatriots. In spite of his country's neutrality, Tatnall, a Southerner, decided that blood was thicker than water and, coming through the heaviest of fire, ran his barge alongside the boat where Hope was lying wounded, and the 'neutral' American sailors helped the reduced British crew to man their guns. The British force had then to withdraw, having completely failed in its object. The landing party was also withdrawn, having suffered 430 casualties.

General Sankolinsin's prestige was enormously enhanced by his victory over the foreign barbarians. This affront to British and French prestige by an Asiatic nation, which was refusing to honour its treaty obligations, led to a military alliance between the British and French. They determined to send to China a force sufficient in strength and numbers to impose, by arms if necessary, the terms of the 1858 treaty.

The British and French Governments agreed that a combined force of 10,000 British and 7,000 French troops be despatched to China as soon as possible. The French contingent was to sail direct from France to Shanghai. The British army would collect at Hong Kong and was to come mainly from India, but with detachments from Britain and the Cape of Good Hope. The Prime Minister, Lord Palmerston, left the military arrangements for the expedition to Sidney Herbert, the Secretary of State for War, and the political to the Foreign Secretary, Lord John Russell. Lord Elgin had been appointed to deal with the diplomatic affairs of the Second China War in

1856; he now received further instructions from the Foreign Secretary to act as plenipotentiary to the forthcoming expedition.

The overall military command of the Allied Army was given to Lieutenant-General Sir Hope Grant. Grant was a tall, dour, lean Scot, a cavalryman, who had served in the 9th Lancers with great distinction and whose powers of leadership had been especially noted during the recent Mutiny in India. He had had little formal education, was fairly inarticulate, but had learnt the lessons of warfare in the hard school of practical experience. He had seen much active service, having fought in the First China War and in both the First and Second Sikh Wars, as well as in the Mutiny. His common sense and intuition, combined with excellent eyesight and strong powers of endurance, enabled him to assess situations very rapidly and often with considerable originality. He was very courageous, and sometimes his personal courage led him to be extremely daring in action. His only reading was his Bible, for he was a deeply sincere and committed Christian, and his relaxation was found in playing and composing for the 'cello. He was particularly skilful at handling his own arm, the cavalry, and he was to put this to good effect in China, where the cavalry were to play a major role. Grant, though a strict disciplinarian, was essentially a soldier's soldier. He was, as a result, loved by all ranks.

He wrote from Lucknow to the Duke of Cambridge at the War Office in London on 23 January 1860

to express my most grateful acknowledgment for the honour conferred upon me by Her Majesty in placing me in command of the force going to China, and I trust that my conduct may be such as to meet with Your Royal Highness's approval. I shall pay attention to your wishes and I shall keep you fully informed on all subjects relative to the war in China. I am fully aware that the position in which I am placed with regard to the French force will be one of some difficulty, and as I strongly feel the necessity of keeping in cordial terms with our allies, Your Royal Highness may depend on my doing all in my power to continue the good understanding which at present exists between the two nations.[1]

4

The French contingent was to be commanded by General de Montauban. Sidney Herbert, in writing to Queen Victoria, commented that he had seen

a letter from Colonel Claremont stating that General de Montauban had been selected by the Emperor of the French to the command in China, with special reference to his conciliatory character and bearing. He is said to be a man of ability and a good practical soldier. The charges affecting his private character being more properly due to the avarice of his wife, who entered into illegitimate pecuniary transactions with the native chiefs in Algeria.[2]

Lord John Russell gave Lord Elgin his instructions, which were to enforce the terms of the Treaty of Tientsin, to obtain an apology for the events of 1859, and to secure the payment of an indemnity to cover the expenses incurred by the Allies. Russell pointed out that in order to obtain these minimum terms it might prove necessary to occupy some part of the Chinese mainland, and if Lord Elgin could also manage to persuade the Chinese to cede the peninsula of Kowloon opposite to the island of Hong Kong, that would be an added advantage. Sidney Herbert instructed Sir Hope Grant in similar terms, and by January 1860 the composition of both the French and British contingents had been agreed. Napoleon III was sending an increased force of some 7,600 men, made up of 5,800 infantry, in seven battalions, three batteries of field artillery and one battery of mountain guns. There were two companies of engineers. The only cavalry was a small escort of fifty men for General de Montauban, and the French provided themselves with no transport at all.

The British Force was to consist of two infantry divisions of two brigades each and a cavalry brigade. On 9 February 1860 it was proposed from Calcutta that the British element should be increased to 16,500 men:[3]

23rd Company, Royal Engineers	120
2nd Company, Madras Sappers and Miners	270
1st King's Dragoon Guards	400
Fane's Horse	356
Probyn's Horse, 1st Punjab Cavalry	400

8/11 Battery, Royal Artillery	201
8/14 Battery, Royal Artillery	159
7/13 Battery, Royal Artillery	203
7/14 Battery, Royal Artillery	182

(Three of the above were horsed field batteries.)

3rd Regiment of Foot (The Buffs)
31st Regiment of Foot (East Surreys)
44th Regiment of Foot (Essex)
60th Regiment (King's Royal Rifle Corps)
67th Regiment of Foot (Hampshires)
87th Regiment of Foot (Irish Fusiliers)
99th Regiment of Foot (Wiltshires)

8th Punjabis
11th Punjabis
15th Punjabis
19th Punjabis
Loodhiana Regiment
Lucknow Regiment
2 Regiments from the Bombay Presidency
1 Regiment from the Madras Presidency

TOTAL

Engineers	390
Cavalry	1,156
Artillery	745
British Infantry	7,000
Indian Infantry	7,200
	16,491

Herbert issued instructions to Grant from London in January 1860, telling him that the fleet, under Admiral Hope, was to be reinforced, and that two batteries of field artillery were to be despatched from England, making their way to Hong Kong via Egypt, together with a battalion of the Military Train, which would make the long sea voyage via the Cape of Good Hope. In addition an infantry battalion, the 2nd Regiment of Foot (The Queen's), would be joining the force from the Cape. Two of the field batteries were to be equipped with the newly issued Armstrong breech-loading rifled guns, and the remainder with smooth-bored nine-pounders. The rest of the force would come from India, and consist of five regiments of British foot, one regiment of British cavalry, three batteries of British artillery and a company of British engineers. In addition there would be two regiments of Indian cavalry, and five battalions of Indian infantry with a company of Indian engineers. All these troops were to be in addition to the regiments already serving in China.

Sir Hope Grant informed the Duke of Cambridge of the various staff appointments that had to be made:

The force altogether when it is made up will be very efficient. The Staff Lord Clyde has appointed to serve in China is excellent. Colonel Stevenson, now at Hong Kong, is to be Deputy Adjutant General. Colonel Kenneth Mackenzie and Colonel Ross, whom you may remember in the Crimea, are to be in the Quarter Master General's Department. Colonel Haythorne, of the 1st Royals in China, is to be the Chief of the Staff, a most excellent Officer. And I shall pay attention to Your Royal Highness's wishes regarding Colonel Foley, and appoint him to be with the French, when I arrive in China. I believe it is also Lord Clyde's intention that he shall hold that appointment. The two Major Generals to command Divisions are Sir John Michel and Sir Robert Napier. The former I am not acquainted with, but I hear he is a good Officer. The latter I know well and I think another choice could not have been made.[4]

In January 1860 Major Dighton Probyn VC took over command of the 1st Sikh Irregular Cavalry at Lucknow, just at the time that rumours were spreading that a force was to be sent to China. Immediately the entire regiment volunteered for this service. There were some men who were unfit for active service, and these were weeded out. Probyn also brought in volunteers from other regiments, as well as a number of old soldiers with whom he had served in the Mutiny and whose promotion he had secured in the Oudh Police as a reward for faithful service. Every man he recalled came, all of them giving up their promotion and re-enlisting as sowars under Probyn, their old chief. On 28 January Grant was still commanding at Lucknow, and on that day he received a telegram saying, 'Pass

7

before you 1st Sikh Irregular Cavalry – Probyn's – and ascertain from each man individually his willingness to volunteer for service in China. Each man to sign or seal a paper. Communicate result without delay.' Grant had Probyn's paraded before him at his quarters, and on the three mile march from their cantonments the men cheered themselves the whole way. Every single man of the regiment signed the paper as he was asked. They then returned to their lines cheering again the entire way. A number of horses were cast and remounts brought in from a draft supplied by the 4th Light Cavalry. On 9 February orders were received to proceed to Calcutta for embarkation. Probyn's marched across country by forced marches, and covered the 600 miles from Lucknow to Raniganj in eighteen days. En route at Benares the 12th Lancers, who were about to return to Britain, made over, by special permission, a hundred Arab horses to Probyn's. At Raniganj, Probyn's was taken by rail to Calcutta, and on 10 March Lumsden, a staff officer in the 2nd Division, minuted in his notebook: 'Went and met Probyn, just come in with his regiment, the 1st Sikh Cavalry, good looking men and well horsed. We will see more of them by and by no doubt.' Probyn's and Fane's Horse, as irregular Indian cavalry regiments operated under the '*silladar*' system, whereby each man owned his own horse. At Calcutta both Probyn's and Fane's Horse lost their *silladar* status for as long as they were on active service in China, and now the British Government took over responsibility for equipping the regiments and for their horses. Neither regiment reverted to the Indian *silladar* status until their return to India at the end of the campaign.[5]

The 1st King's Dragoon Guards were stationed in Southern India at Bangalore within the old Madras Presidency. On 1 March 1860 fifty-eight men joined the regiment from the 12th Lancers, who were returning to Britain, and on the same day orders arrived for a wing of the regiment to proceed on service to China. The following day 14 officers and 312 men, together with 313 horses marched to Madras for embarkation. The Colonel of the KDG was Lieutenant-Colonel Pattle, but he was appointed to command the cavalry brigade in China and so the

KDG wing, comprising four troops, was under the command of Lieutenant-Colonel Sayer.[6]

The 44th Foot (Essex) were also stationed at Madras, in Fort St George. Lieutenant-General Sir Patrick Grant, who was the Commander-in-Chief of the Madras Presidency, specially recommended that the 44th be selected for active service in China because he had formed an extremely high opinion of them during their two years at Fort St George under his command. The 3rd Foot (The Buffs) and the 99th Foot (Wiltshires) were both stationed in the vicinity of Calcutta, and embarked for Hong Kong from that port. The 2nd Foot (The Queen's) sailed direct from the Cape of Good Hope to Hong Kong. The 31st (East Surreys) had only arrived in Poona in February 1859, where they were equipped for the first time with khaki tunics and wicker pith helmets for the hot season, retaining the traditional red jackets for the colder weather. The 2nd Battalion of the 60th and the 67th (Hampshires) were both stationed in India, the latter at Barrackpore. All these regiments were warned for active service in China by January 1860. Among the Indian infantry, the 15th Punjabis were at Gwalior, and on 1 December 1859 the regiment was inspected by Sir Robert Napier, who was to command one of the infantry divisions in China. When a call was made for volunteers for service in China, the entire regiment offered its services, and on 16 January 1860 commenced its march for Calcutta. They reached Cawnpore on 31 January, and from there they travelled to Allahabad by train and then to Raniganj by bullock cart, and so from there by train to Calcutta, which the two wings reached on 22 and 24 February respectively. On 5 March the Regimental Headquarters with two Pathan and one Punjabi Mussulman company embarked for Hong Kong on the transport *Minden*, whilst the three Sikh and two Dogra companies sailed in the *Punjab* and the *Lord Dalhousie*. Cholera broke out during the passage and twenty-two men died.[7]

Probyn's Horse embarked at Calcutta on 19 March in eight 'first-class ships of about 1,000 tons each, reaching Hong Kong by the end of the month'. The King's Dragoon Guards embarked 'A' Troop on board the sail transport *Frank Flint* at Madras on 19 April, with 'G' Troop and Regimental Headquarters on another sail transport, the *Sirius*, the same day. The Headquarters officers were Lieutenant-Colonel Sayer, Captain Wingfield, Lieutenant Greaves and Vetinerary Surgeon Thacker. 'B' Troop sailed in the sail transport *Trimountain* on 6 May, and 'F' Troop followed in the sail transport *Eastern Empire* on 15 May, both having embarked the previous day. Lieutenant-Colonel Pattle, KDG, who was to command the Cavalry Brigade, sailed from Madras on 21 April.[5,6]

The 44th Foot also embarked for Hong Kong at Madras on 31 January, when five companies under the command of Lieutenant-Colonel MacMahon went aboard the transports, followed on 3 March by the Regimental Headquarters under Colonel Staveley. The 44th were a strong regiment, embarking 35 officers and 1,076 other ranks. The men of the King's Dragoon Guards and the 44th were both unfortunate in one respect. On 12 February the regimental families of the service troops of the King's Dragoon Guards, consisting of 53 women and 67 children, arrived in Madras from Britain when the men selected for China were preparing to embark – some one month, and the rest two months later. So after one long separation the families were almost immediately committed to another. The 44th were even more unfortunate, for their regimental families arrived in Madras from England after the first five companies had already left. These women and children had to stay in Madras and make their lives on their own, without even the comfort, afforded to the KDG families, of being greeted and settled in by their menfolk.[6,7]

SOURCE NOTES

1 Royal Archives, Windsor Castle, RA VIC ADD MSS E/1, 2531.
2 Royal Archives, Windsor Castle, RA VIC ADD MSS E/11, 258.
3 Allgood, Lieut. G., *China War 1860*, Longmans Green, 1901.
4 Royal Archives, Windsor Castle, RA VIC ADD MSS E/1, 2531.
5 Boyle, Major A. C., *History of Probyn's Horse*, Gale & Polden, 1929;
Notebook of Captain P. S. Lumsden, National Army Museum; Maxwell,

Captain E. L., *History of the 11th King Edward's Own Lancers*,
A. C. Curtis, 1914.
6 Records of the King's Dragoon Guards, Regimental Museum of the 1st
The Queen's Dragoon Guards, Cardiff; Belfield, E., *The Queen's Dragoon
Guards*, Leo Cooper, 1978.
7 Carter, T., *Historical Records of the 44th, or East Sussex Regiment*,
W. O. Mitchell, 1864; Haswell, J., *The Queen's Royal Regiment*, Hamish
Hamilton, 1967; Blaxland, G., *The Buffs*, Leo Cooper, 1972; Langley, M.,
The East Surrey Regiment, Leo Cooper, 1972; Wood, H. Fairlie, *The King's
Royal Rifle Corps*, Hamish Hamilton, 1967; Atkinson, C. T., *Regimental
History of the Royal Hampshire Regiment*, vol. 1, University Press Glasgow,
1950; Kenrick, Colonel N. C. E., *The Story of the Wiltshire Regiment*, Gale
& Polden, 1963; Gibson, T., *The Wiltshire Regiment*, Leo Cooper, 1969;
Historical Record of the 20th Infantry (Duke of Cambridge's Own),
Brownlow's Punjabis, Swiss & Co., 1909.

2

The Imperial Chinese Government was beset with internal unrest. The regular Tartar army tried to exercise control over the vast distances involved but throughout the nineteenth century had to contend with peasants who had left the land and banded together, sometimes as bandits, sometimes in patriotic groups or in secret societies, and sometimes under local warlords. During 1860 two groups in particular were causing the Imperial Chinese Government a great deal of trouble. The Tai-Pings and the Boxers exploited the xenophobic tendencies of the Chinese, were bitterly anti-foreign, and were in considerable strength around Canton and Shanghai. Because the British base was to be established in Hong Kong, in the south of China, it was in the Allied interest to keep that area as peaceful as possible, whilst the expeditionary force moved on Peking in the north. The Tai-Pings were especially active around Canton and Hong Kong, and the threat of an Allied invasion of the north encouraged the rebels to challenge the Imperial troops there, who were in any case badly led.

Sir Hope Grant arrived in Hong Kong from Calcutta on 13 March 1860 and wrote to the Duke of Cambridge on 27 March:

Poor China is at present in a most wretched condition. The Imperial troops in the neighbourhood of Canton have been beaten by the rebels, or rather *banditti*, and if it were not for our troops the town would probably be plundered and destroyed. People at Canton seem well disposed towards us, and to be aware of the protection afforded by our troops. In the narrow streets of this large city, crowded with population, our European intruders walk in perfect security. The [Chinese] Governor-General, who resides at Canton, is apparently anxious to give every encouragement to our remaining there. He has

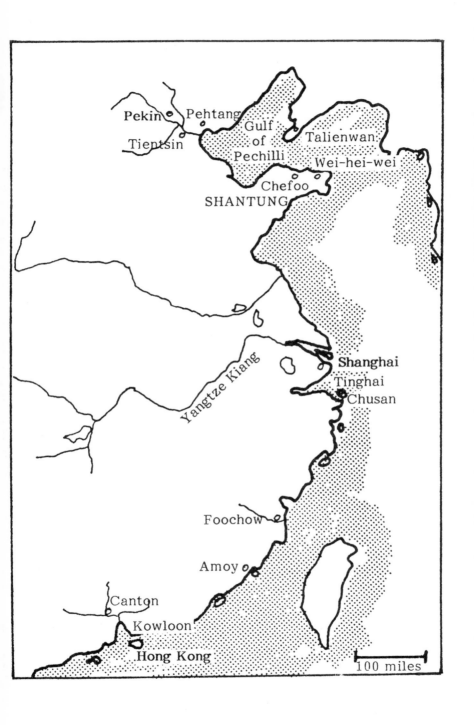

Pekin
Pehtang
Tientsin
Gulf
of
Pechilli
Talienwan
Wei-hei-wei
Chefoo
SHANTUNG

Yangtze Kiang

Shanghai
Tinghai
Chusan

Foochow

Amoy

Canton
Kowloon
Hong Kong

100 miles

even given us a lease of the Kowloon promontory, [which] as Your Royal Highness is aware, lies within three quarters of a mile from the town of Victoria, and in a military point of view is of the greatest importance to Her Majesty's Government, as it completely commands the town and harbour . . . The Governor General willingly acceded to the payment of £160 p.a. rent with the power of retaining it as long as we pleased . . . The 99th Regiment has arrived. A wing of the 44th – a wing of the 31st and the 3rd Bombay Infantry also.[1]

The leasing of the Kowloon peninsula was indeed important, for the rocky island of Hong Kong was not an ideal gathering point for a large expeditionary force. The regular British garrison of Hong Kong at that time consisted of the 1st Foot (Royal Scots) and the 87th Foot (Irish Fusiliers). In 1860 Victoria on Hong Kong island was looked upon as one of the unhealthiest stations; the mass of the island blocked it from the prevailing southerly breezes and also at night helped to retain the heat of the day. On the other hand Kowloon was open to the southerly breeze, and gave room for the troops to encamp as they arrived. Lord Elgin had received instructions to annex Kowloon if necessary, but the troubled internal state of the country around Canton led the Chinese Governor-General to agree to a lease in the expectation that the presence of British troops on the mainland adjacent to Canton would give the local population a confidence they surely lacked, and might also serve to discourage the rebels from approaching too near to Canton itself.

Grant told the Duke of Cambridge on 27 March that

It will prove a much more healthy situation for troops from it being open to the south west monsoon, from which Victoria is shut out. It also has excellent ground for artillery and Brigade practice. I have accordingly encamped there the wings of the 31st and 99th Regiments, which keeps them from the temptations of Victoria. It gives them healthful exercise . . . I visited Canton for two days last week. I inspected the barracks and the positions held. I had a review of the troops, all seemed in good order. I have directed 3 regiments, a battery of artillery and a portion of engineers to be left there, one European and two native regiments being the regiments.[2]

He further reported that he would 'appoint on my departure

Colonel Crawford of the Bengal Artillery to the command of Canton and Hong Kong, giving him the rank of Brigadier General'.[1] On 5 May he confirmed these arrangements:

I arranged everything with regard to the occupation of Canton. Rebels or banditti have been increasing lately much in the neighbourhood of Canton, and the mandarins are in great fear of their advances on the city. I have left one strong European Regiment, the 87th, two Bombay Regiments and a Battery of European Artillery. This appears to give the people confidence, and as long as we remain in possession, I think the town will be safe. I have also left a Depot Battalion of Europeans at Hong Kong, and one strong Regiment of Madras Infantry, 130 Artillerymen and some Engineers. The whole under command of Brigadier General Crawford, who is quartered at Canton, and also appears an energetic, good Officer.[2]

The two native regiments from the Bombay Presidency were the 3rd and 5th Bombay Native Infantry. In addition to the battery of artillery and the engineer detachment, a strong body of military police was added to this holding force. All the commanding positions around Canton were held, with a number of gunboats supporting them in the river and with an additional reinforcement of French marines. The 21st Madras Native Infantry were given the role of providing the garrison for Hong Kong island. As the troops of the expeditionary force itself started to arrive they were organised into two infantry divisions and one cavalry brigade.

Grant's second-in-command was to be Sir William Mansfield, and his appointment had caused the Queen to raise an eyebrow. Herbert wrote to Her Majesty on 17 December 1859:

Mr Sidney Herbert presents his humble duty to Your Majesty and has had the honour to receive Your Majesty's note on the subject of the rank to be conferred on Sir William Mansfield while serving on the Staff in China, and commanding the Infantry Division under Sir Hope Grant. Sir William Mansfield was so appointed with a view in case of accident, of having on the spot an Officer capable of succeeding to a command of a delicate and difficult nature. Mr Sidney Herbert must crave Your Majesty's indulgence if he was in error in thinking that in the case of officers appointed to the Staff, it is the privilege of the General Commanding in Chief to take Your

Majesty's pleasure on such appointments. Mr Herbert trusts that the appointment may meet with Your Majesty's approval, and that the public service in India may not suffer by the postponement of the period at which Sir William Mansfield will take up his appointment as Commander-in-Chief at Bombay.[3]

Grant wrote from India in January:

I have just received a communication from Mr Sidney Herbert, viz., that Sir William Mansfield is to go to China in command of the Infantry Division under me, and that two extra regiments are to be sent out, and Lord Clyde has ordered the 2nd Battalion of the 60th and the 87th Regiments.[4]

The 1st Infantry Division was to be commanded by Major-General Sir John Michel, and it comprised two brigades. The 1st Brigade was commanded by Brigadier-General Staveley, promoted from command of the 31st Foot. In his brigade were the 1st Foot (Royal Scots), who were part of the Hong Kong garrison; Staveley's own regiment, the 31st Foot (East Surreys); and the Loodhiana Regiment of Sikhs. The 2nd Brigade, under Brigadier-General Sutton, was made up of the 2nd Regiment (The Queen's), which had come direct to Hong Kong from the Cape of Good Hope; the 2nd Battalion of the 60th (King's Royal Rifle Corps); and the 15th Punjabis, who arrived in Hong Kong at the end of April and were at once encamped at Kowloon. The 1st Division had also one company of Royal Engineers, under Lieutenant-Colonel Fisher, and two batteries of the Royal Artillery, Lieutenant-Colonel Barry's and Captain Desborough's.

Major-General Sir Robert Napier was given command of the 2nd Infantry Division. The 3rd Brigade consisted of the 3rd Foot (The Buffs) from Calcutta, the 44th Foot (Essex) from Madras, who camped at Kowloon, and the 8th Punjabis. The 44th furnished detachments to the Chinese Coolie Corps under Lieutenant Howorth, and a number of specially picked men were posted to the Corps on a permanent basis as orderlies. The 4th Brigade had the 67th Foot (Hampshires), who had landed at Canton on 23 October 1859 with a strength of 34 officers and 805 men. The winter in South

China had been cold, but the Hampshires had been quartered in huts, which in spite of the severity of the weather had helped to reduce to twelve the numbers of those who died, with another twenty sick enough to be invalided. In February 1860 a draft of 200 reinforcements reached the 67th from Britain, and even when some sixty men had been detached to serve in the Military Train, and with the military police to be left behind in Canton, the regiment was still able to parade more than 800 men for service in the north.[5] The 99th Foot (Wiltshires), from Calcutta, disembarked in March and went into camp at Kowloon. The third regiment of the 4th Infantry Brigade was the 19th Punjabis. The 2nd Division's artillery was made up of two batteries, Captain Govan's and Captain Mowbray's, with Major Graham's company of Royal Engineers.

The Cavalry Brigade was commanded by Brigadier-General Pattle, from the King's Dragoon Guards. Luckily, the three cavalry regiments had all brought their horses with them from India, as had the batteries of the Royal Artillery, for it proved extremely difficult to procure adequate horseflesh in China. All the cavalry horses, too, arrived in excellent condition. However, the British Consul in Amoy had managed to purchase 110 Chinese ponies, who turned out to be the hardiest of all the animals acquired locally, including those bought in Japan. Two troops of the Left Wing of the King's Dragoon Guards arrived in Hong Kong on 15 May, but the other two troops did not reach there until 19 and 29 June, and the following KDG details not until the middle of July.[6] Probyn's Horse reached Hong Kong at the end of April, losing seventeen horses en route, and was immediately stationed at Kowloon. Fane's Horse were not so fortunate; they had been embarked in flat-bottomed lighters and were towed by paddle-steamers all the way to Hong Kong. The country-bred horses of Fane's did not take easily to this method of transportation, but even so only fourteen had been lost, all from a bout of influenza, by the time the paddle-steamers puffed their way into Hong Kong on 16 May after a two-month voyage. Two native officers and fourteen men had died of cholera.[7] Sir Hope Grant wrote of the Cavalry Brigade:

The two irregular cavalry regiments were really magnificent. They were composed of fine, handsome men – Sikhs – becomingly dressed, well mounted, and commanded by two excellent officers, Major Fane and Major Probyn, both of whom I had known well in India during the Mutiny. The King's Dragoon Guards was also one of the finest regiments in the service, and altogether I had reason to be proud of my little cavalry force. It was commanded by Brigadier Pattle of the King's Dragoon Guards.[8]

A small siege train of the Royal Artillery, under command of Major Pennycuick, was allotted to the expeditionary force, together with a battery, of mountain guns from Madras and some 250 Madras Sappers and Miners.

On 27 March Sir Hope Grant wrote to the Duke of Cambridge, worried that he had failed to contact the French General:

I have not yet seen M. de Montauban, from whom I received a letter today stating that he does not intend returning to Hong Kong. I have deferred my departure from this till I should have seen him, otherwise we might have passed one another en route. I was happy to find he approved of our intentions, and that he intends to go north as soon as possible to form a depot. We shall therefore be able to commence active operations in good time.[1]

Because of the difficulty of obtaining forage locally, all of which had to be imported, mostly from Bombay, it was decided to cut down on the number of animals to be taken by the expedition. To compensate for this shortage of animal feeding stuffs, a large corps of Chinese coolies was enlisted to carry the baggage of the army. Major Temple of the Indian Army was given command, and enlisted this corps at a rate of pay of nine dollars or £1. 17s. 6d. a month, together with the issue of two suits of clothes and rations. These were generous terms for the time, but even so Major Temple had great difficulty in recruiting anything but the dregs of the population. It seemed that a rumour had got around that the British would place the Chinese coolies between themselves and the

18

Imperial troops to act as a shield against the Chinese fire. This was given added credence when the seconded sergeants from the British regiments tried to bring some order into chaos by drilling the coolies, with bamboos over their shoulders. The people of Canton and Hong Kong could not believe that such a force, all dressed in the same uniform, and being drilled by British infantry sergeants, was not intended for fighting purposes. The uniform consisted of a Chinese jacket and trousers, the jacket inscribed in front and behind with a circular line, the coolie's individual number and the number of his company, with a black line separating them. The men went barefoot, but wore a flat bamboo hat with the letters 'C.C.C.' painted in the front, standing for 'Chinese Coolie Corps'. Those who were able to speak a little English were promoted to the ranks of lance-corporal, corporal and sergeant, their rank being denoted by the requisite number of white stripes painted on one sleeve. It was said that when this Corps left Hong Kong, the incidence of theft on the island diminished overnight.

Major Temple drew most of his British officers and NCOs from the Royal Marines, although the Regiments of Foot also sent some men. The British officers and NCOs wore a double white stripe down the sides of their trousers for this service.

The battalion of the Military Train had arrived and should have been able to take on all the arrangements for transport. Unfortunately the Military Train showed such incompetence that it had to be split up into three divisions, one of which was sent off to Japan as a Horse Transport Service, in order to try to buy horses and cattle for the force. One of the difficulties was that some members of the Military Train had been trained and used as dragoons in India during the Mutiny, and they expected and longed still to be employed as cavalry and not on transport duties, which they considered to be beneath their dignity. The Commissariat overall was put in the charge of Mr Bailey, who was efficient and a Commissariat Officer of great experience. He co-ordinated the work of the Military Train, the Chinese Coolie Corps, some Filipinos from Manila, and bullock-drivers from Bombay and Madras. But whenever hard work had to be done, it was the Chinese coolies who cheerfully and willingly sweated and carried enormous loads, whatever the weather and the conditions; they even carried to the troops when they were in action. As Cantonese from the south of China their feelings were only of satisfaction as they later watched their northern brethren suffer defeat. Their one failure was in the way they stole, looted and pillaged from their fellow countrymen at every opportunity. But they also showed the stoicism of their race; when one coolie was condemned to death for a particularly bad crime, he looked at the gallows, grinned, and then helped the hangman with the noose.

Grant had been concerned at certain inequalities of pay:

I have found it necessary to issue an order directing 2d per diem to be paid to each man as compensation to assimilate the pay to the Indian rates. Everything here is excessively dear, and it appears to me hard that the Officers should be placed upon (the higher) Indian pay, and the men upon (the lower) English.[2]

The French contingent assembled at Shanghai, starting to arrive in the port during the middle of May. The French, coming direct from France, brought no transport or animals with them. The bulk of their force consisted of five battalions of infantry, but the four batteries of artillery and, to a lesser extent, the two companies of engineers required both transport and horses, which were not available locally. This caused a long delay while the French tried to purchase ponies from Japan, but even when these had been secured, they had to be broken in to work in gun teams. Sir Hope Grant visited his French colleague in Shanghai, and at once realised that they had arrived totally unprepared for the realities of service in China. He told the Duke of Cambridge:

Whilst at Shanghai, in the course of conversation General de Montauban stated that he found great difficulty in procuring ponies and horses. We had at the time 170 ponies collected at Shanghai, and I at once offered to let him have them, paying the same price they cost us. He most readily accepted them, and seemed very thankful, but afterwards, having consulted Heads of Department, he wrote to me to say he found the expense too great, and declined taking them. I said of course it would not make the slightest difference, that I should be only too glad to take them back. I fear, however, if the French go to work in this economical manner, they will not be ready for active operations till it is too late. Ponies would draw their light guns well, but the harness alone will require great attention, as it has been made for full-sized horses. This ought to have been done long ago.[2]

By the time the British were ready to commence operations, the French had still acquired only 114 out of the 600 horses they needed to draw their artillery. Added to these difficulties, General de Montauban, though a soldier with some experience, was not the easiest of colleagues, always ready to take offence at real or imagined slights. Furthermore the alliance was not popular with the troops, who had a native and instinctive distrust of 'anything French'. The French, being the smaller force and under the orders of the Commander-in-Chief, Sir Hope Grant, became sensitive about matters of national pride and precedence. Mr Parkes, the British Commissioner at Canton, commented that 'They act in every respect like a drag on the coach. They use our stores, get in our way at all points, and retard all our movements.'

While the British force was assembling at Hong Kong, an ultimatum had been despatched to the Imperial Court in Peking laying down three conditions for the avoidance of hostilities: an apology for the events of 1859 at Taku, the payment of a sum sufficient to cover the cost of the damage then done, and confirmation of the Chinese ratification of the Treaty of Tientsin. Unless a satisfactory reply to all three points was returned within thirty days, the Allies would resort to hostilities. After twenty-eight days a reply from the Imperial Chinese Government was received, but it was considered not to answer any of the conditions satisfactorily. On 5 May Grant reported:

We are now almost quite ready to take the field. Everything has arrived except a portion of the 2nd Queen's, one Battery of the Armstrong Guns, two Squadrons of the 1st Dragoon Guards, one infantry regiment, the siege guns from England, and 1,000 horses and mules from Bombay. Four heavy guns are already here, and we have sufficient horses for our Batteries, as also bullocks for the heavy guns. Our Couly [sic] Corps is made up almost of 4,000, and in a few days we hope to have ponies to the amount of 3,500. Everything is arranged to start our force on the 10th May for Ta-Lien-Whan [*sic*] or Chefoo. General Montauban sends up his force from Shanghai about the same time. It amounts, I understand, to about 6,000 men.[2]

SOURCE NOTES

1 Royal Archives, Windsor Castle, RA VIC ADD MSS E/1, 2619.
2 Royal Archives, Windsor Castle, RA VIC ADD MSS E/1, 2681.
3 Royal Archives, Windsor Castle, RA VIC ADD MSS E/11, 258.
4 Royal Archives, Windsor Castle, RA VIC ADD MSS E/1, 2531.
5 Atkinson, C. T., *Regimental History of the Royal Hampshire Regiment*, vol. 1, University Press Glasgow, 1950.
6 Records of the King's Dragoon Guards, Regimental Museum of 1st The Queen's Dragoon Guards, Cardiff.
7 Maxwell, Captain E. L., *History of the 11th King Edward's Own Lancers*, A. C. Curtis, 1914; Hudson, General Sir H., *History of the 19th King George's Own Lancers, 1858–1921*, Gale & Polden, 1937.
8 Knollys, H., *Incidents in the China War of 1860*, Blackwood, 1875.

3

The Government in London had ordered that a blockade of the northern ports in China should be implemented if hostilities became necessary. It was thought in London that the cutting off of the grain exported from the south of China to the north would help to starve the Imperial Chinese Government into submission. Like many schemes thought out far from the scene of action, this plan was never put into operation. In the first place no one knew the extent to which the grain was carried by various means of overland transport, rather than by sea. Secondly, the effects could well prove to be double-edged, especially if a successful blockade were to encourage the Imperial authorities to harass the European trading settlements at Amoy or Foo-Chow, for it was only possible for protection to be given to the larger northern trading post of Shanghai and to the southern base at Canton. Thirdly, the effects of a blockade would fall most heavily upon the ordinary Chinese people, upon whose goodwill any expeditionary force would depend. It would hardly affect the Imperial mandarins in Peking.

It was felt, however, that an intermediate base, nearer to Peking than Hong Kong, would assist the operation, and would show the Chinese authorities that the Allies were serious. It was therefore decided in London to establish such a base by occupying the island of Chusan, which lay off the mouth of the Yangtse-Kiang river. Chusan had been occupied by the British in the First China War, twenty years earlier.

The troops embarked to make up the garrison of Chusan consisted of the 67th (Hampshire) and 99th (Wiltshire) Regiments, with four companies of the Royal Marines, one battery of the Royal Artillery (Major Rotton's), one company of the Royal Engineers, and 300 men of the Chinese

Coolie Corps, together with a medical and commissariat contingent.

Grant wrote on 25 April 1860 that he had

left Shanghai on the 18th instant, and arrived the following day at Kintang, the appointed rendezvous for the Chusan expedition. The French contingent, and part of the English, did not arrive till the evening of the 20th. On the following morning, the combined squadrons arrived off Chusan, and a flag of truce was sent on shore, with a summons to the Chinese authorities to give up the island without resistance; and to invite the principal military and civil Mandarins to come off to my vessel to discuss the necessary arrangements for giving it up ... You will perceive that the surrender of the island has been happily effected without firing a shot. The town of Tinghai possesses accommodation for about 1,000 men in the joss-houses and large yamuns; but these buildings appeared very damp and unwholesome. The old cantonments, so healthy in our former occupation of 1841–46, have now been completely built over, forming a populous suburb of the town, and extending down to the very water's edge. Owing to this dense population, and the numerous canals and paddy-fields, there is no place to pitch tents. Under these circumstances, I only selected spots for Commissariat and Coal Stores, and the positions to be occupied by the 99th Regiment [Wiltshires] and Royal Artillery; the 67th Regiment [Hampshires] being left on board their transports. Leaving the whole under command of Brigadier Reeves of the 99th Regiment. I quitted Chusan on the 23rd [April] to return to Hong Kong, where my presence is much required.

As I consider that it will be wholly inadvisable from the insalubrious state of the island to make use of Chusan for anything but a Depot for Coals and Naval Supplies, I visited the island of Pootoo on the 24th to see if it could be made available for a Sanitarium. The island which lies to the east of Chusan, is filled with joss-houses, which afford ample accommodation for 3,000 men. Under the circumstances I do not propose to leave more than 500 men at Chusan, which, with the French garrison, will be amply sufficient.

I cannot conclude this despatch without alluding to the assistance I received from Mr Parkes of the Consular Service, who volunteered his services as Interpreter. In an operation of this sort, it is difficult to overestimate the services of the Officer who acts as mouthpiece of the Commander; and it is to Mr Parkes' intimate acquaintance with the manners and language of the Chinese, that I attribute the speedy settlement of the surrender of the island, effected in a few hours, at a period when time is of great importance.[1]

There was another practical disadvantage about Chusan. When the transports anchored off Kintang, the local tide was so strong that it proved impossible to row against it. This nearly resulted in a tragedy, when some officers of the 67th Regiment decided to explore ashore and on their return were caught in an ebb tide which carried their boat out to sea. They were only saved because another ship, which had been similarly caught, had managed to drop anchor in their path and they were able to grab a line from it.

In writing to the Duke of Cambridge, Grant was more explicit:

The island of Pootoo which is only a short distance from Chusan is in my opinion and that of the Doctor who accompanied me in every way better adapted for a Sanitarium, and it is also equally well situated as a Depot for the Commissariat. Bullocks and sheep can be bought there from the mainland with as much ease as to Chusan. There is also a great advantage this island has over the other that no town is built upon it, which makes it much more difficult for soldiers to procure liquor. Admiral Hope perfectly agrees in all this with me. In a letter from Lord John Russell we are directed to take possession of Chusan, but I do not conceive for a moment Her Majesty's Government would wish me to occupy an island which would cause great mortality amongst the men.[2]

While the 67th (Hampshires) were aboard their transports lying off Chusan, the officers and men of the 99th Regiment (Wiltshires) left on the island , under command of James Day, thoroughly enjoyed the six weeks of their stay there before being recalled to join the main force. They were quartered in the joss-houses of Tinghai; the men had a quiet time, whilst the officers enjoyed a round of parties with iced champagne, gin, and sherry and soda to cheer their spirits, together with many shooting expeditions across the island. The Chinese military mandarin in charge invited Captain Hart Dunne and other officers to a banquet, which consisted of twenty-seven courses, followed by tea, brandy and opium. Hart Dunne and a colleague were asked to arrive two hours before the other guests and were entertained to tea, sherry and cheroots until the formal banquet started at 7 p.m. with the arrival of the other officers.[3]

The good working relationship with Admiral Hope was welcomed by Grant, for at an earlier stage he had had his misgivings. At the end of March he had written:

I have had an interview with Admiral Page, who tells me a Vice-Admiral is to be sent out to replace him. This is done, I presume, to put the French Navy on a footing with ours, as at present the French General seems to have entire command over the Navy. Admiral Page is a gentlemanlike man, but Admiral Hope, I find it is necessary to treat him with caution.[4]

By 5 May, however, it was the French Admiral Page who was also giving him cause for concern:

The conference which took place on board my ship, the *Granada*, and at which Admiral Jones, Admiral Page and myself were present together with the Chief Mandarins of the island [Chusan]. I cannot help stating that the manner of Admiral Page towards these two unoffending gentlemen was overbearing and uncalled for, and I did not think that it was at all courteous towards the Officers of Her Majesty's Service present. I am happy, however, to find that he is no longer the principal naval authority with the expedition. A nice Admiral has been sent out by the Emperor of the French.[2]

Grant, having returned to Hong Kong, determined to move his force north to Shanghai as soon as possible. Any start was dependent on the end of the north-east monsoon, as it was not possible to tow transports against the prevailing current. By the end of May the wind was expected to veer to the south-west and the expedition could then get under way; and it was indeed the end of May when Admiral Hope considered that the weather was sufficiently settled for a start to be made. Probyn's Horse and Fane's Horse, together with the batteries of the Royal Artillery, were embarked in the cavalry transports on 30 May, and the following day the men-of-war steamers set out, taking the horse transports in tow by twos and threes. That night the wind veered again to the north-east and continued to blow hard for the next two days, forcing the ships to put back into Hong Kong. The north-east monsoon had already taken its toll of some of the shipping. The French steam transport *Isère* struck a rock near Amoy and foundered; the British steam transport *Assistance* also hit an uncharted rock when steaming close to the shore and went down with £10,000 worth of stores. A third accident occurred when the French ship *La Reine des Clippers* caught fire at Macao and was burnt out, with the loss of all the winter clothing for the French troops and some 600 tons of coal.

While waiting in Hong Kong, the two batteries of the Royal Artillery, equipped with the new Armstrong guns, had been putting in some practice. It was the first time that a breech-loading rifled field-gun had been used on active service, and there was intense interest in its capability. A target was placed out to sea, and the accuracy of the guns in ranging and hitting the target was remarkable. However, the older muzzle-loading artillerymen were doubtful about the intricacies of the new breech mechanism and indeed the new lead-coated segment shell, together with the delicate fuse, later gave disappointing results in action. Some men were actually killed during the campaign by the lead-coating stripping from the shells in flight and hitting the infantry in front of the guns.

By the end of the first week in June the weather had moderated sufficiently to allow another attempt to be made to tow the transports north to Shanghai, and then on to Talienwan in the Gulf of Pechilli, which had been selected as the jumping-off point for the landing at the mouth of the Pei-ho river. Though there were steam vessels available there were not enough to carry the whole force, and so sailing ships had also to be employed; therefore plenty of time had to be allowed. The fleet set sail from Hong Kong on Friday, 8 June. The final composition of the Expeditionary Force was:—

	Officers	*Men*	*Horses*
King's Dragoon Guards	8	190	185
Probyn's Horse	17	446	433
Fane's Horse	15	347	327

	Officers	Men	Horses
Royal Artillery	50	1,515	747
Madras Mountain Train	7	168	39
Royal Engineers	11	224	
Madras Sappers & Miners	8	245	
Military Train	28	260	
2nd Battalion, 1st Foot, The Royals	28	539	
1st Battalion, 2nd Foot, The Queen's	28	617	
1st Battalion, 3rd Foot, The Buffs	27	823	
31st Foot (East Surreys)	30	970	
44th Foot (Essex)	25	940	
2nd Battalion, 60th Rifles	30	772	
67th Foot (Hampshires)	32	818	
99th Foot (Wiltshires)	22	584	
8th Punjabis	15	763	
15th Punjabis	15	943	
19th Punjabis	19	463	
Chinese Coolie Corps	14	264	
	419	10,491	1,731

Bruce Tulloch of the 1st Royal Scots, one of the two British battalions which made up the original garrison of Hong Kong, described the journey:

The transport which was to take the Royals to the north was an Aberdeen clipper of 1,000 tons, a small ship to take a whole regiment; but deaths and invaliding had, notwithstanding the addition of a fine draft from England, brought down the strength of the battalion to 500 rank and file. Even then it was a tight fit, but, as we were going on active service our little discomforts were not worth troubling about. When the first division of transports, all sailing ships, was ready, the wind was against us, so we had to beat out, tack and tack, and, as in the days of the old war, we had two men-of-war as convoy. They were powerful paddle-wheel frigates, and went with us not as a protection against any possible enemy we might meet, but to assist any ship which might come to grief. The transports kept pretty well together until we got through the Formosa channel, and then, a gale coming on, we lost sight of the rest of the fleet, and made our way straight for the rendevous – viz., Talienwan Bay.

To a regiment which eighteen months before had come to China in a sailing ship from Gibraltar, life at sea was no novelty. The Officers of the Calcutta flagship, the first man-of-war allowed to come into a Japanese harbour, gave us some very interesting accounts of their experiences with the then unsophisticated Japs, in whose eyes everything European, especially naval buttons, was of wonderful value. Our voyage was uneventful.[5]

Sir Hope Grant left Hong Kong in the steamer *Granada* with his headquarters on 11 June and made for Shanghai, which he reached on the 16th. Before leaving he had received a report that the people of Shanghai were in a panic, due to the approach of the rebel Tai-Pings; the civil and military mandarins at Shanghai had asked for protection, and so the gates of the city were occupied by Allied soldiers. Grant reported:

As I deemed it advisable to strengthen the present force at Shanghai, I ordered the regiment of Loodianah [*sic*], which was to have been left at Kowloon, to embark for Shanghai, there to be stationed for the present. They will arrive in the course of a few days.[6]

He had also changed his mind about retaining Chusan:

With reference to my former letter intimating the possibility of Chusan being abandoned as a Military Station. After communicating with Her Majesty's Minister it has been determined to retain that island; a force of 500 men from the British portion of the garrison, the remainder having sailed for the north on the 10th instant. I am happy to add that the troops at Chusan have been, throughout, remarkably healthy. Quarters for the troops have been comfortably fitted up, and sanitary measures enforced, and I receive the most favourable reports of the place.[6]

Grant and his staff put into Shanghai for a few days on their way north. Garnet Wolseley, a lieutenant-colonel on the staff, commented on the

dirt, filth, and every conceivable stench abounding everywhere. Hung around the walls in conspicuous places were small wooden cages containing each a human head; some of these had been hanging there since the place had been retaken from the rebels, others were of much more recent date, being the heads of pirates, and those who had been convicted of assisting in the kidnapping of coolies by the Americans and French, about which there had been such serious commotions.

Our mercantile community were uneasy about their property; and all knew that their lives would be in danger if the rebels poured down upon the place. At the earnest entreaty of the Chinese officials, a battalion of Royal Marines was landed and quartered in those places around the settlement and city, where they might command the approaches to the place and at the same time find accommodation.

The north gate, a joss-house on the Soochow creek, and the Ningpo guild-house were occupied, and fitted up at the Mandarins' expense as barracks for our men. A house was hired within our settlement as quarters for 200 men with Officers. This being a central point, it was strengthened by three small guns; the French also held a gate of the city, and occupied some houses within the place. The Loodianah [sic] Regiment of Sikhs was ordered up from Hong Kong, and the 11th Punjaub [sic] Regiment was subsequently added to the garrison.[7]

The time that the staff spent in Shanghai was not entirely concerned with military preparations. The British traders offered generous hospitality, and Grant played his 'cello. The wife of the French Minister, Madame de Bourboulon, smoked cigars, much to the astonishment of some of the British staff. On 16 June a planning meeting was held between Grant and de Montauban, the French Commander. It was agreed that the French should land south of the Taku forts and that the British should establish themselves further east, so that the two contingents could attack the forts from the flank and rear. However, there would have to be delays, because the French were still not fully equipped and were particularly short of horses. In the meantime the British would set up their advanced base at Talienwan and the French would establish a similar base at Chefoo on the Shantung peninsula.

Chefoo had a small harbour which was well protected from bad weather. The Shantung peninsula was able to provide the French with plenty of cattle and with the much sought after draught animals, but water was scarce and the harbour was too small to accommodate both the French and British fleets. Colonel Fisher of the Royal Engineers had made a reconnaissance, earmarking Talienwan for the British and thinking that

Wei-hei-wei on the west side of the Gulf of Pechilli might also provide a possible advanced base.

On leaving Shanghai, Grant visited both Chefoo and Wei-hei-wei on his way to Talienwan. On arrival at Talienwan he wrote to the Duke of Cambridge on 30 June,

having visited Wei-hei-wei and Chefoo on the Shantung promontory on my way up. At Wei-hei-wei there is a small walled town containing a Civil and Military Mandarin and about 2,000 inhabitants. They appeared civil and well-disposed, and upon being asked if they would provide supplies for our force stated that as far as lay in their power they would, but that they had not much to give except goats and fowls. There also appeared a great deficiency of water, no streams being in the neighbourhood, and only sufficient to supply the inhabitants. The country near the shore was mountainous and there was not much cultivation, and the harbour does not hold accommodation for more than 12 or 15 ships.

At Chefoo the French have encamped their troops, and mean, I believe, to make it a Depot. It is in the same way badly off for water, but by digging wells, they procure a sufficient supply for drinking, and the sea water is used for working purposes. General Junim, who is in command, informs me that all the French Infantry have arrived at Chefoo amounting to 5,600 men, but I regret to say, states that it will be impossible for the force to be ready by the 15th July, as their artillery is so deficient of means, and that the artillerymen had not yet reached. They have obtained a sufficient number of ponies from Japan, but as yet only 114 have arrived at Chefoo, and they have not disembarked their guns. The ponies appear strong and serviceable, but have not yet been tried in draft, and General Montauban is also not expected, at the soonest, to leave Shanghai till the 2nd or 3rd July.[8]

Colonel Wolseley had also visited Chefoo and was impressed by the French arrangements:

Our allies were living in their *tentes d'abri*. Although latterly the weather was warm there was very little sickness in their army. By covering over their little tents with matting, they succeeded in making them endurable, which, without some protection of the kind, they never could have been under such a sun. A considerable amount of timber lay about in piles ready for use, which the French sappers quickly turned into planking, with which they constructed comfortable quarters. Their camp was very compact and neatly laid out, and order seemed well kept around. I never saw so many men on duty in a small place before – I should fancy that nearly one third of their whole force was continually on guard. By this means all plundering was prevented, and the country people, in consequence, gained confidence, so that very soon after our allies arrived, a good market was established. A considerable number of fine mules were also obtained by their commissariat at prices ranging from twenty to forty dollars. Some of these animals were extremely vicious, and most of them very intractable, until after a time they became accustomed to their new owners, but all were in good condition.[7]

SOURCE NOTES

1 Royal Archives, Windsor Castle, RA VIC ADD MSS E/1, 2669.
2 Royal Archives, Windsor Castle, RA VIC ADD MSS E/1, 2681.
3 Kenrick, Colonel N.C.E., *The Story of the Wiltshire Regiment*, Gale & Polden, 1963.
4 Royal Archives, Windsor Castle, RA VIC ADD MSS E/1, 2619.
5 Bruce Tulloch, Major-General Sir Alexander, *Recollections of Forty Years' Service*, Blackwood, 1903.
6 Royal Archives, Windsor Castle, RA VIC ADD MSS E/1, 2735.
7 Wolseley, Lieut-Colonel G. J., *Narrative of the War with China in 1860*, Longman, Green, Longman & Roberts, 1862.
8 Royal Archives, Windsor Castle, RA VIC ADD MSS E/1, 2748.

4

By the middle of June the troops were starting to arrive at Talienwan, on the Manchurian peninsula and near the present site of Port Arthur, now the modern port of Luta. The Talienwan bay offered an excellent anchorage for the large British fleet. The bay was about nine miles long from north to south and some thirteen miles deep from east to west. The shoreline was made up of a series of smaller bays: Victoria Bay to the south east; Hand and Pearl Bays, side by side on the north east; Odin Bay, a few miles to the south; and Bustard Bay, between Odin and Pearl Bays. Because of the shortage of water it became necessary to distribute the troops; the 1st Division under command of Sir John Michel was placed to the west of Victoria Bay, the 2nd Division under Sir Robert Napier was at Hand Bay, whilst the Cavalry and Artillery were at Odin Bay, where there was the best supply of water for the horses. The Military Train was encamped partly at Bustard Cove and also at a stream near to the 1st Division's camping ground at Victoria Bay.

Sir John Michel and some of the troops of the 1st Division were the first to arrive. Bruce Tulloch of the 1st Foot (Royal Scots), who was in the first transport, described the scene:

The country round the bay, open undulating ground, was a first rate place for the concentration of a large force, the only drawback being a rather limited supply of water. My Company happened to be sent on shore a day or two before the others for landing camp stores, etc. The British force at Talienwan, in consequence of the water difficulty, had to be spread out on both sides of the bay; but as the Chinese forces were a long way off at Taku, we could safely make our own arrangements[1]

The 44th (Essex) Regiment and Brownlow's Punjabis arrived on 16 June, but did not land for some days until the various camp sites had been determined. When Brownlow's did eventually disembark on 27 June, they and the men of the 44th were set to digging wells. The 67th (Hampshires) and the 99th (Wiltshires) were brought up to Talienwan from Chusan. On 10 June they set sail, the 99th leaving 200 men as garrison at Chusan, and joined the main convoy arriving at Talienwan on 16 June.[2]

Robert Swinhoe of the Consular Service travelled with some of the King's Dragoon Guards from Hong Kong.

On the 9th June the *Lightning* steamed round to Deep Bay, on the other side of Hong Kong, and, taking the *Sirius* in tow, proceeded up the coast. The *Sirius* had on board Brigadier Pattle and fifty five troopers of the King's Dragoon Guards, with their horses. My fellow passengers on board were mostly Officers on the General's Staff, for whom there was not room on board the *Granada*. And a curious group we were: there was just that amount of disagreeableness that usually occurs among Englishmen who are strangers to one another, and yet are fully aware of the appointment and position that each holds; in a word, there was no conviviality.

A northerly gale met us pretty sharply; and finding it difficult to proceed with the *Sirius* in tow, our Captain wisely ran to shelter on the lee of the Lam-yit islands, where we found several other vessels of the northern expedition also anchored. In this delightful anchorage we were detained until the 16th. Several of the ships in harbour with us contained Sikh cavalry, so that it was necessary to send the syces ashore to procure forage. These gentry had not been well drilled in the rights of 'meum' and 'tuum', and therefore it did not surprise us to hear sad stories from the natives of the fresh supplies they had stolen, or of the injuries they had inflicted . . . On the 16th June the gales abated, and we again put to sea. At sundown on the 21st June we arrived at Talienwan.[3]

Three more troops of the King's Dragoon Guards disembarked at the cavalry camp at Odin Bay on 4 and 5 July, and the fourth troop arrived on the 14th.[10]

Sir Hope Grant reported that

On my arrival at Talienwan, which is about 80 miles distant from Chefoo, I found the whole of the British troops anchored in the harbour, with the exception of about 120 men of the 1st Dragoon Guards, all in good health and ready for active operations. The bay is

34

large and the country around possess considerable advantages over the Shantung promontory. Several running streams have been found, and though small, contain sufficient water to supply the Fleet and Army, which is a matter of the greatest importance from the number of ponies and horses we have. The harbour is also large enough for any number of vessels.[4]

The troops having arrived at Talienwan, there were further delays. The French at Chefoo were not ready and were still looking for an adequate supply of horses. This delay added to the unpopularity of the French with the troops. As one of Fane's officers commented, 'If in our previous alliance in the Crimea the French cavilled at our want of preparation for war, the boot was certainly on the other foot now.'[5] Bruce Tulloch of the 1st Foot complained:

It will hardly be credited that on the 1st July, when the whole of the British Army had arrived at Talienwan Bay and was ready to start on the campaign, the French, at Chefoo, had only 114 unbroken Japanese ponies collected for their field artillery, for which some 600 were necessary. The consequence was that the expedition had to be delayed a whole month simply waiting for the French to get their transport ready.[1]

Grant continued the story:

In consequence of the delay we are called upon to make, I have found it necessary to disembark the troops and have placed them on three different sides of the Bay. The artillery, cavalry and ponies at the east, where there are small streams, and with the two Divisions, one at the north, and the other at the west, where water has been procured by digging wells. The country is mountainous and the population are very civil and apparently well disposed, but are in great dread of their Mandarins, which prevents them freely bringing in provisions. Markets however have been established at each of the posts, where a certain amount of supplies are to be obtained, and which I trust will increase when confidence has been established.

I intend forming a Depot at Odin Bay, at the east point of the bay, where the artillery and cavalry are placed, and giving up all idea of the Shantung promontory. At present the climate is everything that could be wished for, the thermometer ranges from about 70 to 85, and there is usually a cool breeze blowing. The hot weather is said to commence at the beginning of July and to last until the end of

August, but as yet the weather has been most agreeable, and anything but hot.[4]

When the troops first landed they found large quantities of oysters along the shore, which although small had an excellent flavour. Many, both the officers and men, indulged too freely and suffered violent stomach pains. Bruce Tulloch wrote:

The second night I was in a bad way with an attack very like cholera – originated, I thought, very possibly by the Talienwan oysters. When at its worst, a violent squall with a heavy sea set in, which brought my tent down. I had just strength left to place some stones on the canvas to prevent its being blown or washed away, and crawled up the beach to a small hut, where I had rather a bad time until daylight brought our surgeon ashore. We lost two men from similar attacks, and then the complaint, whatever it was, ceased.[1]

Surgeon Rennie reported to the principal medical officer concerning the health of the soldiers ashore:

A large amount of sickness prevailed. The symptoms closely resembled those which prevail at Hong Kong – fever, dysentery. Yet the position was remarkably healthy; there was no intemperance as intoxicating liquors cannot be obtained beyond the ration. The Army has been weeded of its weakly and sick at Hong Kong, and the troops at the first were selected in India as men of known robust health. The lowest amount of sickness occurred in the 99th Regiment, and I observed that that regiment alone is furnished with the Indian tent, the rest of the infantry use the bell tent.[6]

Grant, the strict disciplinarian, insisted that all provisions bought from the local Chinese had to be paid for; there was to be no plundering. Bruce Tulloch recalled how he went 'with another subaltern to cater for our mess, and buying at a farm a nice little black pig, which would not be driven, so we had to lash it to a pole, and then carried it squealing, shoulder high in triumph back to our camp'.[1] This policy soon started to pay off, as the Chinese gained confidence and returned to their villages.

Grant was optimistic about supplies generally:

Our Commissariat promises well. We have 60 days at present on board ship, and the Navy [has] 90, without taking into consideration the fresh supplies which the country will afford. From Canton and

Shanghai, to which places steam vessels are constantly to run, Commissary General Turner informs me that large numbers of bullocks and sheep are expected, and vessels will also be sent to Nagasaki in Japan for the same purpose.[4]

There was little disciplinary trouble with the British and Indian soldiers, but the same could not be said of the Chinese Coolie Corps. These Chinese were southerners from around Canton who could not speak or understand the Mandarin dialect which was used in the north. They stole and looted wherever they could, and no amount of punishment seemed to curb their activities. However, Wolseley related how

The Coolie Corps proved itself of great use, working most cheerfully and well; eighty, however, deserted one night, of whom we heard nothing, until, a few days subsequently, six of the party returned in a most pitiable condition, having, according to their story, been beaten and ill-treated by the inhabitants, some of the party had been beheaded and all of them imprisoned. Although we lost men by this circumstance, it was of great ultimate benefit, as it showed all the others what they might expect from their northern countrymen if they left us, and made them consequently all the more anxious for our success.[7]

Robert Swinhoe wrote:

Captain Con of the 3rd Buffs, having been nominated Provost-Marshal, took up his quarters with me. The Coolie Corps and the Punjaubis [sic] were objects of the most frequent complaints. They plundered the natives right and left, but some wholesome chastisement, severely administered, soon reduced them to obedience.

Even if this view soon proved over-optimistic, Swinhoe was more realistic than Surgeon Rennie over another temptation besetting the British soldier:

Though the natives were slow in bringing in fresh provisions, they soon found out the failing of the British soldier for drink; and but few days had elapsed before we found liquor in the camp. Proclamations in Chinese were, therefore, issued, to warn the people, but to no purpose: the cane of the provost-sergeant was the only effectual remedy.[3]

A Royal Marine who harboured a grievance against one of his officers shot at him. He was court-martialled and condemned to death. Thomas Bowlby, the *Times* correspondent, related how in early July the sentence was carried out:

Punctually at one o'clock a boat from every vessel in the fleet assembled around the flag-ship. Just astern of her was moored the *Leven*, the vessel on board of which the act was committed. A large open space was kept around her and at a signal from the Admiral the boats approached the *Leven* in two equal divisions. A rope was passed out on either side of her to which they strung themselves, the bowman of each boat having gone on board. The rigging of every ship was then manned by all hands to witness the execution. Punctually at half-past one the prisoner was brought out, stripped of his uniform. He looked deadly pale, but his step was firm and he showed no sign of fear. A rope was passed around his neck. The signal was given, and in a couple of seconds the bowmen from the boats had run him up to the fore yard arm. There a loop was loosed, and he fell with a heavy drop at least six feet. A couple of struggles and all was over. For half an hour his body was left swaying in the wind, an example to all beholders. He died penitent and made a full confession to the Roman Catholic Priest who attended him. The only reason he assigned for the attempted murders was that he had been falsely accused of stealing brandy. He hoped his fate would be a warning to others. There is no doubt that he was astonished at the sentence; for, as Lieutenant Hudson was not dead, he expected seven years' transportation only. But clemency in such a case would have been madness, and it may be hoped that the swift and speedy justice, whereby the crime has been followed, will check any disposition to mutiny.[8]

Another difficulty arose from the Chinese addiction to opium, the trade in which was one of the main causes of the war. Swinhoe relates how

The Chinese Coolie Corps were much addicted to opium, which formed another subject of complaint. The young Officers commanding the Corps, having heard, no doubt, that opium had a most deleterious effect upon the system and disinclined men to bodily exertion, thought it their duty to request the General to interdict the free circulation of this article among the coolies. I was desired forthwith to forbid the natives from bringing it into camp; but fortunately the prohibition was disregarded. The drug found its way somehow among the coolies, whom you might see smoking it at all hours of the day. Our people, like many other well-meaning philanthropists, had forgotten that where the practice of indulging in the drug had become a habit, it was not so easily laid aside. The privation of the drug, instead of invigorating the men and fitting them for work, would in mosts cases have had a contrary effect: the habitual smokers would have pined away, and eventually died.[3]

Lord Elgin reached Shanghai on 19 June, and after a few days there came on to Talienwan, where he arrived on 9 July. Grant had an early conference with him.

After having seen Lord Elgin and heard his views about the war, I, at once, proceeded to Chefoo to hold a conference with General Montauban and Admiral Churnor. Admiral Hope was unable to go in consequence of an injury he had received on his leg. From the great difficulty I had expected in getting a sufficient supply of water for the force under my command, I wrote a letter to General Montauban on my first arrival at Chefoo, and requested General Gunin to give it to him. I offered, though much against my will, to lend the French either Artillery or horses to enable us to secure the Pehtang. He refused to comply with my request. Though General Montauban says that we are only bound to effect the landing at the points agreed on, the earliest on the 15th and at the latest on the 25th July, he would not hold himself bound to my day for starting. The French are, however, doing their utmost to get ready, and I trust the delay will not be of long continuance.

After his conference with the French, Grant was more cheerful: 'I found that the French had got a sufficient number of ponies for artillery purposes, and also all their artillery-men.'[4]

Wolseley noted that the time waiting for the French to complete their preparations was taken up with inspections and reviews for the troops; during off duty hours there were games for the men and walking expeditions for the officers. Camp life was not without its own perils. Captain Lumsden, the Quartermaster General of the 2nd Division, and Captain Gordon of the Madras Sappers and Miners were crossing Victoria Bay when their boat capsized. Captain Lumsden survived by being a strong swimmer, but Gordon drowned. On another occasion a party of officers of the 60th wandered too far from camp and were chased by a group of Chinese villagers armed with gongs and spears.

Thomas Bowlby

sailed to the Cavalry Camp, and saw General Crofton, then commanding, and Major Hay, his Brigade Major. The latter accompanied us throughout all the camp, consisting of all the Artillery, the KDG, Probyn's Horse and Fane's Horse. The horses are in excellent health; there are but 40 sick out of 1775. The Indian Cavalry Regiments laid on a display of tent-pegging, Probyn led and Fane was second. Both went near but neither succeeded, their horses being out of practice. Next came a Sikh at a tremendous pace, shouting at the top of his voice, with body extended, and spear close to the ground. He carried away the peg amid great cheering. It was afterwards carried off four or five times in succession. A small piece of cucumber was then put at the end of a stick. Probyn rode at it at full gallop and sliced off the top. Fane followed with an equally good cut, and a third officer completed the cutting, the stick having never been moved.[8]

A few days later, on 13 July, an inspection of the Cavalry Brigade was laid on for the benefit of the newly arrived Lord Elgin and the French General de Montauban. De Montauban and his naval commanders had arrived that day on board the *Forbin*. Bowlby described the scene:

We found the troops drawn up on the beach, a Battery of Armstrong guns on the left, the KDG, and Probyn's and Fane's Horse. It was a lovely sight, with the vast varieties of hue and colour – the dark blue of the Artillery contrasted well with the light blue tunics and red turbans of Fane's Horse; while Probyn's blue black tunics and turbans were relieved by the scarlet uniforms of the King's Dragoon Guards. A salute of nineteen guns welcomed Lord Elgin, and two of thirteen guns each were bestowed on the French General and Admiral.[8]

Grant wrote:

I was glad to show off the other day to General Montauban our Artillery and Cavalry force, and I am sure you would have been pleased with their appearance. There were about 1,000 men on parade; handsome, fine looking fellows, well dressed and turned out, and their horses in beautiful condition. General Montauban stated that it was a sight to see in Paris or in London, but one he did not expect to see so far from home. The Infantry force is also in excellent order, very healthy and their condition very good.[9]

The 67th Regiment (Hampshires) confirmed Grant's satisfaction, having only twelve men sick; and when the whole force re-embarked for the landing on the mainland of China, the 67th mustered 29 officers and 752 men. Grant held several more conferences with the French, and just when it appeared that operations could commence, on 19 July the French asked for a change of plan. The original plan allowed for the British to land north of the Pei-ho river and for the French to disembark to the south. However, as Wolseley commented,

The French Navy, having made a careful reconnaissance of the coast near Chi-kiang-ho, on which they had previously fixed as their point of disembarkation, found, they said, that there was not sufficient water for their vessels, and that consequently they must land at Pehtang with us. This was naturally a great disappointment to us all, and, I suppose, to our allies also.[7]

More conferences were held. It was finally agreed that both armies would set out on 26 July and would meet at a point some twenty miles south of the Pei-ho.

Embarkation of the cavalry and artillery horses, together with the transport animals, began on 21 July and was concluded by the afternoon of the 24th without a single accident. The King's Dragoon Guards embarked on the 23rd, but left behind at Odin Bay some details under Major Slade. Grant had decided to establish a depot at Odin Bay, where the cavalry and artillery had camped, and four companies of the 99th Regiment (Wiltshires), together with 417 men of the 19th Punjab Infantry and 100 artillerymen, were left there as a garrison. In addition, some 200 British and 100 Indian sick were left behind to recover, and hospital accommodation for 440 British and 500 Indian casualties was prepared for the force. During the time at Talienwan two officers had died (one being Captain Gordon, who drowned) and twenty-eight British men. Most of the dead came from the 1st Regiment (Royal Scots), whose health had been undermined by their garrison tour in Hong Kong. The Indian troops lost only six men dead.[2,10]

The Infantry embarked on 24 July, and on the 26th the fleet set sail. Bruce Tulloch described the scene:

The departure of the expedition from Talienwan Bay, in glorious weather at the end of July, was a magnificent sight, with close on ninety sailing merchant transports in two lines, and steamers placed on the flanks as repeating ships, to signal orders and see that the skippers of the merchant vessels kept proper intervals. Our line was led by the *Cambrian*, a fast-sailing 40-gun frigate. Occasionally a warning gun would be fired, and a transport's number hoisted to keep station. As the cost of the powder was charged against the delinquent skipper, none offended a second time. When well out to sea, we met the much smaller French transport fleet, and together we swept along to that part of the coast beyond where the Pei-ho comes out, and anchored.[1]

The combined fleet was carrying some 20,000 men in three lines of ships, the first two lines being British and made up of 173 vessels; in the third line were the French, with 33 ships. Wolseley commented:

Looking around on that brilliant naval spectacle, I could scarce realise the fact of being some 16,000 miles from England. It was a sight well calculated to impress everyone with the greatness of our power, and to awake feelings of pride in the breast of the most stony-hearted Briton. The magnitude of our naval resources was brought forcibly home to the mind of everyone who saw such a vast fleet collected in the Gulf of Pechilli, without in any way interfering with our commerce elsewhere.[7]

SOURCE NOTES

1 Bruce Tulloch, Major-General Sir Alexander, *Recollections of Forty Years' Service*, Blackwood, 1903.
2 Carter, Thomas, *Historical Records of the 44th or East Essex Regiment of Foot*, W. O. Mitchell, 1864; *Historical Record of the 20th Infantry (Duke of Cambridge's Own), Brownlow's Punjabis*, Swiss & Co, 1909; Atkinson, C. T., *Regimental History of the Royal Hampshire Regiment*, vol. 1, University Press, Glasgow, 1950; Kenrick, Colonel N. C. E., *The Story of the Wiltshire Regiment*, Gale & Polden, 1963.

3 Swinhoe, R., *Narrative of the North China Campaign*, Smith, Elder, 1861.

4 Royal Archives, Windsor Castle, RA VIC ADD MSS E/1, 2748.

5 Hudson, H., *19th King George's Own Lancers, 1858–1921*, Gale & Polden, 1937.

6 Selby, John, *The Paper Dragon*, Arthur Barker, 1968.

7 Wolseley, Lieut.-Colonel G. J., *Narrative of the War with China in 1860*, Longman, Green, Longman & Roberts, 1862.

8 Bowlby, C. C., *An Account of the Last Mission and Death of Thomas William Bowlby*, private circulation, 1906.

9 Royal Archives, Windsor Castle, RA VIC ADD MSS E/1, 2773.

10 Records of the King's Dragoon Guards, Regimental Museum of 1st The Queen's Dragoon Guards, Cardiff.

5

The fleet which had gathered in the Gulf of Pechilli consisted of men of war and transports. The transports were loaded in the order in which it was intended that the troops should land. The 2nd Brigade of the 1st Division, commanded by Brigadier-General Sutton, was to carry out the initial landing, and the regiments of the brigade were accommodated:

	Men	Horses	Ship
2nd Regiment (The Queen's)	400	2	*Bosphorus*
	220	1	*Burlington*
60th Rifles	424	2	*Alfred*
	378	2	*Indomitable*
15th Punjabis	626	3	*Bentinck*
	216	1	*Viscount Canning*
	102	1	*Forerunner*
Captain Desborough's battery, Royal Artillery (8 guns)	55	40	*Rajah of Royal Cochin*
(3 guns)	55	40	*Euxine*
Rotton's Rocket Battery, RA	50		*Merchantman*
Lieut-Colonel Fisher's Company, Royal Engineers	94		*Arracan*

The 1st Brigade of the 1st Division was commanded by Brigadier-General Staveley, and was to land next from the following transports:

	Men	Horses	Ship
1st Regiment (Royal Scots)	569	4	*Macduff*
31st Regiment (East Surreys)	392	3	*Hugomont*
	308	4	*Australian*

	303	3	*Mars*
Lieut-Colonel Barry's Battery,	110	80	*Pioneer*
Royal Artillery (6 guns)			
Half-company, Royal Engineers	50		*Arracan*

The men of Major-General Sir John Michel's 1st Division were ordered to land with three days' cooked rations, fifty-six rounds of ammunition, water-bottles full, and with greatcoats, haversacks and canteens. The men who formed the advance party in gunboats were to wear on their backs their folded greatcoats with canteens attached; those who followed in the troop boats were to have their greatcoats folded but not worn. Each landing boat was to have a due proportion of officers, and the commanding officers of battalions and their regimental adjutants were expected to be the first to step ashore.

A memorandum from the Headquarters ship *Granada* reminded all that

It must be borne in mind, that under whatever circumstances the troops land, it is necessary that they form quickly and regularly at once. Officers will, therefore, caution their men (and set the example themselves) that there be no rushing from the boats, which always causes hurry and confusion, and risks the ammunition becoming wet; the soldiers should be distinctly told that their ammunition and firelocks must be kept dry.

It is essential that everything belonging to the soldiers should be placed in a safe place on board the vessels previous to landing, and the masters of transports instructed to have all articles carefully placed in the boats when sent for. One non-commissioned officer and a few men [are] to remain in each vessel for this purpose.[1]

The Cavalry Brigade was to land after the 1st Division, and they had been loaded in the following ships:

	Men	Horses	Ship
King's Dragoon Guards	59	66	*Sirius*
	77	82	*Frank Flint*
	66	64	*Trimountain*
	62	65	*Eastern Empire*
	68	68	*Harry Moore*

	Men	Horses	Ship
Probyn's Horse	51	55	*Lady Ann*
	51	58	*France*
	51	53	*Brandon*
	50	52	*Matilda Atheling*
	74	77	*Ocean Home*
	76	90	*Queen of England*
	49	52	*Nimrod*
	54	58	*Cambodia*
Fane's Horse	67	71	*Voltigeur*
	101	104	*Edith Moore*
	60	63	*Dartmouth*
	58	60	*Clarendon*
	77	85	*Daniel Rankin*
Captain Milward's Battery, Royal Artillery (6 guns)	201	118	*Queen of the East*

The 2nd Division, commanded by Sir Robert Napier was to land later. The men of the division were carried in the following transports:

	Men	Horses	Ship
3rd Regiment (The Buffs)	408	2	*Miles Barton*
	405	3	*Earl of Clare*
44th Regiment (Essex)	353	2	*Athlete*
	316	1	*York*
	286	1	*Imperatrix*
67th Regiment (Hampshire)	538	4	*Tasmania*
	272		*Cressy*
8th Punjabis	270	1	*Dalhousie*
	262	2	*Minden*
	268	1	*Punjaub*
Capt Mowbray's battery,	60	56	*Zuleika*
Royal Artillery	67	54	*City of Poonah*
(6 guns)	68	57	*Elizabeth*
Capt Govan's battery,	97	73	*British Flag*
Royal Artillery	80	74	*Maldon*
(6 guns)	66	40	*Mary Sheppard*
Major Graham's company, Royal Engineers	88	5	*Imperatrix*

Royal Marines	246	2	*Adventure*
Madras Sappers & Miners	251	1	*Statesman*
Mountain guns (20 guns)	219	38	*Michigan*

The Chinese Coolie Corps was carried:[1]

Headquarters Coolies	100	in	*Winifred*
1st Division Coolies	100	in	*Hugomont*
	100	in	*Australian*
	100	in	*Mars*
	100	in	*Bosphorus*
	100	in	*Indomitable*
	50	in	*Macduff*
	50	in	*Malabar*
2nd Division Coolies	100	in	*York*
	100	in	*Athlete*
	100	in	*Earl of Clare*
	100	in	*Tasmania*
	100	in	*Cressy*
	90	in	*Malabar*
TOTAL	1,290		

The fleet had assembled off the Chinese coast, out of sight of land, by 28 July. The 29th was a Sunday and the ships remained anchored in some nine fathoms of water. That evening the gunboats arrived with Chinese junks in tow containing ten days' provisions. The next day the fleet moved in to within nine miles of the shore, so that the coastline was just visible from the mastheads; and that evening the orders for the landing on the following morning were issued.

The morning of 31 July was wet and stormy, the sky overhung by dark clouds, with frequent bursts of torrential rain, and with a heavy sea running. Because of this the landing was postponed until the following day, 1 August, when after a dull start the weather soon cleared and it was decided to take advantage of the high tide at 4 p.m. to make the assault. Wolseley described the scene:

As we approached the mouth of the river we obtained a good view of the town and forts, situated on both banks. This was a strange site for a town; no tree, bush, or even blade of grass was to be seen in any direction; nothing, in short, but mud, which was visible everywhere. Behind the town a wooden gate and bridge led to a causeway, which seemed to stretch towards the Pei-ho. At the bridge there was a party of cavalry, numbering about two hundred and resembling Cossacks.

The landing was to be made opposite the small town of Pehtang, which lay some twenty miles from the mouth of the Pei-ho river and the Taku forts. Pehtang was guarded by two small forts and a wall. Brigadier-General Sutton's 2nd Brigade of the 1st Division provided the assaulting force. On the afternoon of 1 August some 200 men of the 2nd Regiment (The Queen's), with an equal number from the French 101st and 102nd Regiments, and a few Chasseurs of the French General's escort, who were mounted on miserable Japanese ponies, together with one nine pounder gun and a rocket battery, were rowed ashore in small boats, each boat holding about fifty men. The boats made for a spit of land revealed by the ebbing tide, but, when still two hundred yards from the shore, grounded on a mud bank a mile from the forts. The men of the Queen's jumped into the sea, and waded waist deep towards the shore.

Wolseley continues:

There was about a mile of deep muddy flat to be waded through immediately on landing, so there was little of the pomp and circumstance of war about that operation. The first man to jump ashore and lead up the mud bank was the Brigadier. He was an old campaigner well known for his swearing propensities, and famous as a game shot in South Africa. I shall never forget his appearance as he struggled through that mud, knee deep in many places. He had taken off trousers, boots and socks, and hung them over his brass scabbarded sword which he carried over one shoulder. Picture a somewhat fierce and ugly bandy-legged little man thus accoutred in a big white helmet, clothed in a dirty jacket of red serge, below which a very short slate-coloured flannel shirt extended a few inches, cursing and swearing loudly 'all round' at everybody and everything as he led his Brigade through the hateful mire. I remember many funny scenes in my soldiering days, but I never laughed more than I did at this amusing disembarkation.[2]

48

Robert Swinhoe relates:

On reaching the shore a flat of soft, sticky, slippery mud extended across on every side. Through this we waded, sinking ankle-deep at each step. For fully three quarters of a mile did we flounder and struggle before reaching a hard patch of similar mud, evidently covered by the sea during very high tides. Nearly every man was disembarrassed of his lower integuments.

Immediately after the reconnoitring party had effected a landing, the Tartars [cavalry] retreated along the causeway, and the order was given to disembark the rest of the force at once. This was effected, without accident, by five o'clock, not a single shot having been fired by the enemy.

On landing a French Colonel rushed forward with the Chasseurs, and occupied the causeway [which led from Pehtang to the Pei-ho] close to the gate [of Pehtang] on the very spot which had been allotted to the English forces. Sir Hope Grant at once halted his troops, and spoke to General Montauban. In the promptest manner, and without a moment's hesitation, the French General despatched his Chef d'Etat Major, to recall this regiment, which was soon marched along the causeway to its proper position. The English army then advanced, the [60th] Rifles to the right, and the Queen's on the left. They were on an island cut off from the causeway by a deep ditch forty feet wide, through which the tide flowed. In plunged the Brigade, and sank middle deep in the vilest and most stinking slush; but the men struggled gallantly on, and in a few seconds the whole force was on the road.

The sun was sinking fast, as from the causeway we surveyed the position. The bridge and the gate were occupied without delay by 100 Rifles and 100 French, without a shot being fired. Sir Hope Grant was strongly pressed to occupy the town [Pehtang] at once, but he most steadily refused. Evening was rapidly closing into night. So it was arranged that the gunboats should attack at four next morning, and the whole army lay down in the mud on the causeway, and waited for the approach of day.[1]

The men, surrounded by muddy salt water, could find none that was fit to drink. Although they had landed with full water bottles, they had drained these in the exertions of the landing and it was a welcome moment when some of the Chinese Coolie Corps made an appearance with fresh supplies from the ships. During the course of the evening the interpreter from the

1st Division, Mr Gibson, wandered over to Pehtang and found some friendly Chinese who showed him the forts, which they claimed were empty. Gibson reported this to Mr Parkes and Captain Williams, the Deputy Assistant Quartermaster General of the 1st Division, who with a party of the 60th Rifles and the friendly Chinese entered the southern fort to find four Chinese watchmen asleep, but no weapons other than a few wooden dummy cannon in the embrasures. The Chinese showed the officers where the booby-traps had been laid, and the party then returned to the causeway. [1,3]

Bruce Tulloch, who was in the 1st Brigade, which had followed Sutton's Brigade ashore, noted that

The only defence which the enemy's commandant made was of a passive nature, and decidedly Chinese in conception — ground torpedoes of large spherical shells, four in each box, one of which was buried in the mud inside the forts at the foot of the ramps leading to the high cavalier bastions. The shells, by ingenious arrangement, were to have been exploded by the first inquisitive man who might walk up the ramps of the deserted forts. [4]

Later Captain Govan of the Royal Artillery discovered a jar of powder with a lighted slow match stuck in it, and this caused a general order to be issued warning all of the danger of booby-traps. [1]

Next day, 2 August, Sir Hope Grant and de Montauban entered Pehtang, and the town was divided as equally as possible between the French and British troops. Grant made his headquarters under canvas in one of the forts, while the French General set himself up in a large house in Pehtang. The soldiers were moved into the houses of the town, whereupon most of them were ransacked. The French soldiers had no compunction in looting what they could find, and were to be seen wandering about dressed and decorated in Chinese silks and satins. Grant was annoyed by their behaviour:

I regret very much that our troops are thrown so closely in contact with the French. We have been obliged to occupy the town, the French taking one side and we the other. The plunder and robbing that has been committed by them is a very bad example to our men. The officers appear not to try to stop it.

50

The British troops were kept under a stricter discipline, and anyone found plundering was immediately tied up and flogged; the only difficulty was encountered with the Sikh soldiers, who looked upon loot as their fair recompense, but even they were soon brought under control. The livestock, such as it was, quickly disappeared, the British going for the chickens and ducks, with the French slaughtering every pig they could find.[1,2,3,4,10]

On the early morning of 3 August a combined force, under command of the French General Collineau, probed up the causeway towards the Pei-ho and the Taku forts. At 4 a.m. 1,000 French infantry supported by two rifled three-pounder mountain guns and some engineers set off, followed by 1,000 British from the 60th Rifles and the 15th Punjabis, under the command of Brigadier-General Sutton. The force advanced for three miles before coming to a bridge, where a Tartar vedette was posted, but the Tartars galloped away to join a larger body of some 300 Chinese horse in and around some deserted houses. As soon as the French infantry had crossed the bridge the Chinese opened fire with their matchlock rifles and gingals. Collineau ordered his men to deploy and the two mountain guns to come forward, but then a larger body of some 2,000 Chinese cavalry joined their comrades and spread out onto both flanks of the Allied column, threatening to envelop it. As the two guns opened fire, however, the Chinese retired.

The advance now continued, with the French on the right of the road and the British on the left in columns of regiments, until the troops reached a large entrenched camp, surrounded by a crenellated wall, built across the road. A considerable body of cavalry was threatening the British on the left, and so the Queen's were ordered to send forward their skirmishers, who forced the Chinese to retire. When they came to within 1,200 yards of the entrenched camp the men were told to lie down, as the Chinese fire was still heavy. Grant and de Montauban came up, and decided to retire as they had no cavalry ashore as yet to support the infantry and artillery.

Brigadier-General Sutton asked for help in case he was pressed by the enemy on retiring. The Royal Scots and two guns were ordered forward. As the Royal Scots marched along the causeway to support the reconnaissance, they met the few wounded being brought back on stretchers; the going was so muddy that the men had to roll up their trousers above their knees. When the regimental surgeon slipped in a mudhole, he was quizzed as to why he took so much care of a box he was carrying. 'Don't be so cheeky, I may require that box before the day is finished – it contains my amputating knives.' As the troops returned to Pehtang, they were met by the two guns of Desborough's battery of Horse Artillery, who had landed only the night before, and now came up at fine speed, each gun drawn by six horses and making light of the mud.

The Chinese did not follow up the withdrawal, but reports of an overwhelming victory over the foreign barbarians were sent back to Peking. The French had an officer and six men wounded in this engagement, and the British suffered three casualties; most of these wounds were caused by bruising from the weight of gingal shot falling as spent rounds. The gingal was a Chinese weapon new to British troops; it was a type of huge musket, serviced by a team of three men, two of whom supported the barrel of the gingal on their shoulders, whilst the third aimed and fired it. It threw a ball of about one pound weight, and its range depended upon how much powder the crew had the courage to insert, as the weapon had a repeated tendency to blow up in the faces of the crew.[1,3,4]

On 5 August Grant reported to the Duke of Cambridge on the progress so far achieved:

We occupied the forts at the mouth of the Pehtang on the 2nd, without much difficulty, and without firing a shot. The fleet anchored within 10 miles on the 30th, and on the 1st August we crossed the bar to within about 2,000 yards of the forts. They looked formidable, but we afterwards discovered that the guns had been removed to some other place higher up the river, as it was not reported that we should attack them. It was arranged with the Admiral that we should disembark to the south, that the gun boats were to proceed up at night above the forts, and take them in reverse, and that we should make a combined attack at four o'clock in the morning of the 2nd, the Navy firing at the north and we at the south forts. We effected our landing at high water and Your Royal

52

Highness would have been amused to see us, General Officers and all, wading through a mile of sea over a muddy bottom. After a two mile walk we came to a raised causeway, upon which we bivouacked for the night, securing a bridge which led into the town.

I ascertained however that there would be no opposition to our occupying the town, and in the morning of the 2nd we marched into the fort. We were informed that two mines had been placed inside which by walking over, would explode. They were fortunately discovered in large cast iron shells, 16 inches in diameter, buried under ground with a flint cover slightly covered over with earth, and which, when the pressure of the foot was applied to it, would have gone off and probably exploded the powder.

The town is too small for the two forces now in it, and there is not a spot outside where troops could be placed. There is not a drop of fresh water to be got, except what comes from a distance, and which is brought in earthenware vessels by the natives. The only road out of the town is the one we came in by, and two days ago General Montauban and I sent out a force to reconnoitre along it. At about 5 miles out they came upon a large force of the enemy principally crowding in an entrenched camp. They kept up a sharp fire of gingals, and three of our men got struck with spent balls. The Admiral has done everything in his power to land the force quickly, and I trust that by the 7th or 8th, we shall be ennabled to attack their position.[10]

The 2nd Division, under Sir Robert Napier, were still at sea on board their transports. On 4 August orders were received to disembark the troops, and Napier and his staff landed that day.[1] On the 5th the 67th (Hampshires) landed, carrying three days' rations, fifty-six rounds of ammunition and their greatcoats. They were dressed in 'summer frocks', a red serge shirt, and wearing white wicker helmets.[5] The 44th (Essex) followed on 6 August.[6] The cavalry had also started to disembark; the King's Dragoon Guards, with a strength of 13 officers and 313 NCOs and men, together with 339 horses came ashore during the 5th and 6th.[7] What struck Bruce Tulloch

was the workmanlike way in which the blue-jackets landed the horses of the Indian cavalry brought in by the gun boats, with whips and slings on their little foreyards. A horse fully accoutred was hoisted up, swung over the jetty, and dropped ashore on its legs before it knew what was being done to it.[4]

Bowlby wrote:

Late last night [4th] Probyn arrived at Headquarters, and all this morning his horse have been arriving. They are picqueted in the mud, and though rather draggle tailed, both horses and men are in superb condition.[8]

With the troops safely disembarked the next days were spent in landing stores and supplies, and in trying to build up enough material to enable the advance to be made. The engineers had built a number of jetties, which greatly helped the task of getting everything ashore, while the men of the infantry regiments were employed in trying to improve the state of the road. Any attempt to move forward, however, was held up by the slowness of the French in landing their stores; they had few gunboats and were little prepared for active operations under Chinese conditions. In addition the weather was bad and the rain was making the state of the ground very difficult. The sanitary conditions within and around Pehtang were appalling, and the smell of the Chinese town urged a move forward as soon as possible. Bowlby commented on 9 August that 'The cavalry horses are standing nearly knee deep in the rain, which has completely flooded the fort.'[8]

On 9 August Grant sent out a second reconnoitring party, made up of fifty men of 'B' and 'F' Troops of the King's Dragoon Guards and two squadrons of Probyn's Horse. They were under command of Major Probyn, and were sent out to report on the state of the country to the north of the causeway. The cavalry were supported by a hundred infantry, who took up a position two miles down the causeway, in a ruined farmhouse usually occupied by a Tartar cavalry picket. Here they protected the flank of the cavalry as the latter reconnoitred off the causeway. Major Probyn had received strict orders not to be drawn into action, and although several bodies of Tartar horse were seen hovering within easy distance, they were left alone. Probyn's force made a long detour which brought them to within a mile of the Chinese positions at the

Pei-ho. They found out that the country was practicable to all arms, and with plenty of fresh water. Major Probyn was complimented by Sir Hope Grant on his return with this valuable information, and on the fact that not a shot had been fired either at, or by, the cavalry. Grant had the information that he needed in order to make the advance, and by 12 August enough stores had been landed, and the French were ready.[1,3,7,9]

SOURCE NOTES

1 Swinhoe, R., *Narrative of the North China Campaign*, Smith Elder 1861.

2 Wolseley, Lieut-Colonel G. J., *The Story of a Soldier's Life*, vol. 2, London 1903.

3 Wolseley, Lieut-Colonel G. J. *Narrative of the War with China, 1860*, Longman, Green, Longman & Roberts, 1862.

4 Bruce Tulloch, Major-General Sir Alexander, *Recollections of Forty Years' Service*, Blackwell, 1903.

5 Atkinson, C. T., *Regimental History of the Royal Hampshire Regiment*, vol. 1, University Press, Glasgow, 1950.

6 Carter, Thomas, *Historical Records of the 44th or East Essex Regiment of Foot*, W. O. Mitchell, 1864.

7 Records of the King's Dragoon Guards, Regimental Museum of 1st The Queen's Dragoon Guards, Cardiff.

8 Bowlby, C. C., *An Account of the Last Mission and Death of Thomas William Bowlby*, private circulation, 1906.

9 Boyle, Major A. C., *History of Probyn's Horse*, Gale & Polden, 1929.

10 Royal Archives, Windsor Castle, RA VIC ADD MSS E/1, 2786.

6

The Chinese had been encouraged by the reports sent back of their supposed success in repelling the Allied reconnaissance of 3 August. The Chinese Governor of the local province sent to Lord Elgin proposing negotiations, but the Allies had already determined that they would not talk to the Chinese until they had reached Tientsin. Accordingly Lord Elgin declined the invitation. He had been as disturbed as Grant by the French propensity to loot:

This dreadful alliance, what will it not have cost us before we are done with it? The French by their exactions and misconduct have already stirred to resistance the peaceful population of China.[1]

The 99th Regiment (Wiltshires) had been brought over from Talienwan, where they had formed part of the garrison left behind at Odin Bay. They were now left to garrison Pehtang and to guard the stores. In addition one officer and forty men from each regiment remained to look after the regimental baggage, until such a time as it was safe to move it forward. Lumsden, the Deputy Quartermaster General of the 2nd Division, noted that the transport allotted to the cavalry for the advance was to be fifty bullock carts for the sick, and a further twenty-five to carry water for both horses and men.[2]

Grant had agreed with de Montauban that the British and French should lead the advance by turns, and that as the British had the larger continent, they should have the privilege of leading first. On 18 August he reported to Sidney Herbert:

Having secured Pehtang, I commenced landing everything, and having divided the town with the French, we were enabled to get our men, though crowded, under cover. The horses were picqueted in the narrow lanes and streets. Shortly after our arrival, it commenced to rain very heavily, and I don't think it is possible to conceive anything more wretched than the state of the town. The narrow streets became almost impassable from mud, filth and dead animals, which there was no place to bury. And when thrown into the river, the tide was sure to return them to us, and leave them on some muddy banks, where the stench they made was most offensive. The weather cleared up, and having ascertained that a cart track went up the right of the causeway, about 800 yards from the town, I sent a cavalry reconnoitring party on the morning of the 9th to ascertain the way it took, and if it was practicable for Artillery. The Officer in command, Colonel Wolseley, the Assistant Quartermaster General, made his way along it to the right of the enemy's entrenchments, and reported to me that it was possible to move guns along it, and after the first two miles the ground became more sound.

The same afternoon it again commenced to rain very heavily, and the town and country became in a worse state than ever. It appeared to me that remaining in such a position might seriously injure the health of the men, and I accordingly determined, at any risk, as soon as it was possible, to get the troops out and attack the enemy.

On the 11th, I accordingly went to General Montauban and told him my intention of moving out the following [day], but the French General did not seem disposed to think the move was wise or necessary, stating an advance to be impracticable on account of the nature of the ground. I was, however, determined to go, and told him that he might come or not, as he pleased. He said if I went, he must go, but that he would only take a portion of his force.

I reconnoitred the two miles reported to be bad, and found that though muddy, guns could be got through with the help of fascines, which I directed to be laid down immediately, and at 4 o'clock a.m. on the morning of the 12th August (grouse shooting day) I started off the 2nd Division under Major General Sir R. Napier; the Cavalry Brigade; an Armstrong battery; three six pounder guns; and a rocket battery along the road to the right. The guns were dragged through every difficulty, but the waggons stuck, and it was necessary to take the limbers off, and leave the remainder, under charge of a party, behind.[3]

Wolseley describes the move:

The 10th was rainy, and on the 11th we had some slight showers, so that throughout the force the odds were against our moving as intended on the 12th, but when day broke on that date, although the weather was looking threatening, and the clouds hung about in dark masses, yet the rain did not come down. So the exodus from Pehtang, with all its detestable odours, began. It was arranged that the 2nd

Division, under General Napier, should move out along the track reconnoitred by the cavalry on the 9th, and turn the left of the enemy's position, whilst the 1st Division and French advancing along the causeway towards the enemy's front should take their works. All the Cavalry were to accompany the 2nd Division, the ground to our right being admirably adapted for that arm.[4]

Lumsden's notebook for the 2nd Division records: 'Immediately the 67th [Hampshires] has cleared the ground, the cavalry will follow in the following order; K.D.G., Fane's Horse, Probyn's Horse, and 3 guns of Stirling's battery.'[2] The order for the 2nd Division was for an advance guard, commanded by Lieutenant-Colonel Sargent of The Buffs, made up of 200 men of the 3rd Regiment (Buffs), supported by two Armstrong guns of Milward's battery, then the main body comprising the four remaining Armstong guns of Milward's battery, the rest of The Buffs, the 8th Punjabis, the 44th Regiment (Essex), the 23rd Company of the Royal Engineers, with the Madras Sappers and Miners, the Royal Marines, Rotton's rocket battery, and the right wing of the 67th (Hampshires) bringing up the rear with the reserve ammunition, and stretchers. Behind the main body came a rearguard of the left wing of the 67th (Hampshires).[5,6]

Wolseley continues:

The 2nd Division and Cavalry commenced filing across the only bridge, which led to the only road leading out of Pehtang, at four a.m., but as a considerable quantity of rain had fallen between the 9th and the 12th, the ground immediately to the right of the road and close to it was very deep. Indeed, not withstanding all the exertions of the engineers to make a road over it, it was in some places so slushy, that it was only by dint of flogging the horses, and all the gunners working at the wheels, that the difficult task of pulling the Artillery over to the higher and better ground could be accomplished. Three ammunition waggons stuck immoveably, and these we had to leave, taking on the limbers only.

Owing to these waggons sticking in the mud, and the slow progress made by all our troops, and particularly the heavy cavalry, over the deep ground leading from the causeway, the 1st Division could not commence filing over the bridge [out of Pehtang] until a quarter past seven o'clock; the French being somewhat late in

58

forming up, the whole force had not crossed until some minutes past ten, the main body of the French being even then in the town.[4]

Swinhoe noted that the advance was

a fearful trudge for the unfortunate troops, numbers kept dropping out in the line of march, and rested for a while on the side of some grave mound; others, especially the Punjabis, finding their boots an impediment, preferred throwing them away, and tucking up their trousers, pushed boldly on. It was likewise painful to see the cavalry horses struggling on knee deep with their heavily accoutred burdens.[7]

Grant reported that

This force at last got over the difficulties of the two miles of bad ground. It was attacked by a large body of Tartar cavalry, some 3,000, who in the most daring way came up close to the guns. Our Cavalry were let loose upon the Tartars, and they had a hand to hand fight, cutting down about 70 or 80. The enemy behaved very gallantly and under better rulers would make excellent troops. They completely surrounded Sir Robert [Napier's] Division in skirmishing order, and remained about it like a pack of hounds.[3]

The 2nd Division deployed as soon as it had cleared the muddy area, with the Cavalry Brigade protecting its right flank, so that an advance could be made against the left of the Chinese entrenchments. Half of Milward's battery, three guns, were ordered forward, covered on each flank by a company of the Buffs, with a third company behind. The rest of the infantry of the 2nd Division were drawn up in columns of regiments behind, with the other half of Milward's battery and Rotton's rockets protecting the left flank, and Stirling's battery covering the right.

As soon as the troops deployed, a mass of Tartar cavalry trotted forward in a loose order and, sweeping right around the Cavalry Brigade, began to threaten the left wing of the 67th Regiment (Hampshires), who were guarding the Coolie Corps carrying the reserve ammunition, stretchers and medical equipment. The 67th had been armed with the new Enfield rifle and managed to halt the Chinese horse with their accurate fire, but the Tartars merely withdrew some distance and hovered until finally driven off by a company of the 67th sent out in extended order.[5] It was at this point that, with a loud yell, Probyn's and Fane's Horse, supported by two squadrons of the King's Dragoon Guards, charged and scattered the enemy, cutting down numbers of them. This was too much for the Tartars, who turned and fled, pursued for five miles by the Indian sowars and British troopers, until the attacking cavalry were halted by the blown condition of their horses. The Chinese, who were mounted on small hardy ponies accustomed to the terrain, easily outdistanced the British and Indian horses who, having been cooped up on board transports at sea, were at this early stage of the campaign still in a poor condition. The Tartar horsemen behaved with considerable courage, and not even the accurate fire of the Armstrong guns had daunted them.

Stirling's battery supporting the 2nd Division had been making slow progress through the muddy area, and a troop of twenty-five sowars of Fane's Horse under Lieutenant Mac-Gregor had been left behind to escort them. About a hundred of the Tartar cavalry spotted this small party and charged them, 'uttering wild and unearthly cries', and hoping to capture the guns. Stirling managed to unlimber and get off two rounds of case shot; but MacGregor, his escort, as soon as he saw the Tartars heading towards him, led his twenty-five men in a spirited counter-charge against four times his numbers.

One of the leading Sikhs ran his spear right through the body of a Mongol horseman, the head entering his chest and going out at his back. The spear broke in the middle, the Mongol fell to the ground spitted, and never moved a limb. Lieutenant MacGregor singled out his man, and was in the act of spearing him, when another Tartar fired his matchlock within ten yards pointblank. The slugs hit the Lieutenant in five places, three lodging in his chest, two in the forehead. For a moment he was blinded by the fire, which burnt his face, but the work was done. The Tartars dispersed in every direction, the whole affair lasted little more than a minute.[7,8,9,10,12]

Four companies of the 44th Regiment (Essex) were acting as guard to the guns of their brigade when some Tartar horse tried to attack them. The Essex wheeled into line and drove off their assailants with volley fire. Captain Bower of the 44th, in charge of an ammunition escort, also repulsed a charge of Tartar cavalry.[6] Grant had returned to the 1st Division along the causeway:

As soon as I got within about 2,000 yards of the enemy's position, [the entrenched camp in front of Sinho], I managed to deploy a Regiment to the right across the swampy ground, and the French were enabled to do the same to the left, a Battery of Armstrong guns being placed in the centre. We advanced to within about 600 yards of the enemy's entrenchments without a shot being fired, when they opened [fire], to which we returned with great effect. I brought up as soon as possible another Battery of nine pounders and a French Battery, and we opened a fire from these eighteen guns at such close range upon the crenellated walls of the entrenchment that the enemy could not remain, and after half an hour's firing, the place was evacuated.[3]

Brigadier-General Staveley, commanding the 1st Brigade, had led the advance of the 1st Division. Skirmishers of the Royal Scots were sent out to the left, and of the 31st Regiment (East Surreys) to the right. Colonel Barry's battery of Armstrong guns and Captain Martin's battery of nine-pounders opened fire, with a French rifled battery in support on their left and a British and French rocket battery on the right. Bruce Tulloch commented:

In front of us, at a considerable distance from Pehtang, were two earthworks, one on each side of the causeway. As we got near, my Company, which was leading on the right, was extended in skirmishing order; and it was interesting, as we marched forward in silence, to observe the enemy's rammers and sponges tossing about against the skyline, and as soon as we got within range the shot splashed up the mud in grand style. The shot came pretty thick at first, but our artillery soon silenced the enemy. The skirmishers being well forward, our gunners fired over us, but somehow the guns behind made one feel more uncomfortable than those in front. We used rocket-tubes also: fortunately those erratic missiles were well on the flank.

On the right there was a grand spectacle. A large force of Tartar cavalry, certainly some 2,000 or 3,000, rode with wild cheers straight at the 1st Division. The infantry Brigadier in front, instead of receiving them in line, actually formed regimental squares. This sight of our men running into masses greatly impressed the Tartars, who came on most pluckily almost up to the guns, which with the rocket battery were firing hard into them. Fortunately the Sikh cavalry were behind the guns, and then got their chance. Riding into the dense mass, they punished them heavily, and quickly cleared the whole of them off the field.[11]

Probyn's and Fane's Horse, supported by the King's Dragoon Guards, had again charged the Tartar horse, which was threatening the 1st Division, but the Chinese were not prepared to meet a second cavalry charge and beat a hurried retreat. Pensioner Duffadar Nihal Singh of Probyn's noticed that the Chinese seemed to be mainly armed with swords and bows, and he was himself wounded by a Chinese arrow in this engagement.[8] Brigadier Pattle, of the King's Dragoon Guards, now commanding the Cavalry Brigade, had spent his army life with the Queen's regular cavalry and was not accustomed to the more relaxed methods of the Indian Irregular Horse. Probyn, in charging, had taken his whole regiment with him, but had not rallied, and went on chasing the Chinese, with groups of his sowars going after individual parties of the Tartar horse for up to an hour and a half. Lieutenant Anderson of Probyn's Horse, with five of his men and two of Fane's Horse, had been surrounded by some 300 to 400 Tartar horsemen. Anderson was in fighting mood and had killed seven of the enemy, with Sowar Wayeer Khan of Fane's Horse riding beside him until the sowar was himself killed. Sowar Khowajah Mahomed stayed with Anderson and charged the Tartars several times, and then when Anderson was disabled by a sword cut on his arm rushed back to his assistance whereupon Anderson saw him kill four Tartars. Duffadar Berjon Singh of Probyn's became dismounted in a hand-to-hand combat, but refused to leave the field and continued to fight the Chinese on foot until being severely wounded, when his life was only saved by several of his comrades rushing to his assistance. When Pattle sent his aide-de-camp to recall him, Probyn had noted the plight of Anderson. He told the aide-de-camp that he would rally only after he had rescued his men, and without more ado galloped towards Anderson. The Chinese fled, but not before Probyn had killed several of them with his own sword. By this time the sowars' horses were blown, and Probyn complained, 'We got awfully few of them, not more than fifty, the beggars ran so fast.' Later Probyn's men rounded up some 300 Tartar horses, together with 400 sheep, the latter being handed over to the Commissariat. Pattle had complained to Grant about Probyn's failure to obey his orders, and Grant read Probyn a lecture. But he also told Pattle to remember that Probyn and Fane were irregular cavalry, which did not behave in the same way as regulars, and that Pattle might be wise to let them have their heads in future.[12]

Wolseley was watching the advance of the 1st Division from the flank where the 2nd Division had halted:

The guns opened fire upon the enemy's entrenchments, at a range of about 1,000 yards. The enemy stood well for a few minutes behind their mud walls, and discharged their gingals and matchlocks with rapidity, and, very fortunately for us, without any precision. A considerable number of cavalry were in and around their works, when our fire commenced, and it began to tell on them at once. A move was immediately perceived amongst these horsemen, first, by a few leisurely leaving, and then, after a few rounds more, by large numbers bolting as fast as their active little ponies could carry them, so that by the time our infantry had reached the place, the only occupants were dead and dying horses and men. So beautifully precise had been the practice of the Armstrong guns that, in two instances, the men serving large gingals had been knocked over, aim having been taken at them. The French rifled guns were most accurate, their precision being quite as good and their service as efficient.

Some French troops coming up, the whole army now advanced and passed through the village of Sinho, a small place consisting of two long streets, very narrow and slushy. The armies halted at Sinho, the Cavalry and 2nd Division to the southwest of it; beyond this to the south and east of the village were the 1st Division and the French.[4]

Grant summed up the action in front of Sinho:

It was a beautiful field day, the two Divisions coming up at the same time, the one on the enemy's left, the other on his front, doubling him

63

up and taking all his camp. Major Probyn and Captain Fane of the Irregular Sikhs Horse did their work admirably. Our whole loss with both Divisions was two men killed, three Officers and eleven men wounded.[3]

Probyn's and Fane's each lost one sowar killed, Probyn's had two British officers wounded, and six Indian officers, NCOs and men wounded, whilst the King's Dragoon Guards had one trooper slightly wounded.[10,13]

Wolseley had noticed that

About two and a half miles to the south east [of Sinho], the large entrenchments around the village of Tangku were visible, having a long narrow causeway with ditches on each side, leading from our position to it. The country to the north of this causeway was very swampy and quite impassable for all arms, but to the south the ground, although marshy in some spots, appeared sufficiently hard for guns to move over it.

General Montauban was very anxious to advance at once to assault that position, but Sir Hope Grant was desirous of postponing the operation until he had thrown bridges across the canals which separated the roadway and village from the open firm ground to the south of the causeway. [Grant] permitted the French General, who appeared to regard the operation an easy one, to advance alone, keeping, however, a couple of battalions under arms near the causeway to be at hand if required. [These two battalions were the 60th Rifles and the 15th Punjabis.] The guns and infantry of our allies filed down towards Tangku along the causeway until they had approached within the range of their own rifled guns of that place, when their artillery unlimbered and opened fire. The enemy replied gun for gun; but, the range being too great for their pieces, their practice was wild. After a couple of hours thus spent at long bowls, General Montauban seemed convinced of his mistake, and accordingly withdrew his guns and men.[4]

Grant reported that

General Montauban tried to follow up the enemy, after we had driven them through the town, or rather, village of Sinho, but he was obliged to return after having fired some few shots at long ranges at another large entrenched camp which lay on the Pei-ho some 3 miles distant. There was only one narrow causeway which led up to their position, and on which the enemy had guns bearing. I deemed it more advisable to reconnoitre the country before attempting to attack the entrenchment.[3]

Swinhoe visited the Chinese entrenchments before Sinho, which had been taken by the 1st Division and the French. They merely consisted of a long arc-shaped crenellated wall stretching on either side of the road, which passed right through it. Several of the arch-roofed mud huts were disposed about for the accommodation of the Tartar troops, and a very large blue awning set up on poles stood in the centre for the the use of the Mandarin in command of the cavalry, or for Sankolinsin himself. The enemy had no large guns in this position, and appeared to have no infantry at all within its walls. So that both the entrenched camps captured at Sinho were merely strong cavalry outposts.[7]

On 13 August most of the troops were able to rest, whilst the Royal Engineers built bridges over the canals and improved the access across some of the marshes. The heavy baggage had come up on the evening of the 12th, and all the men had been able to spend the time under canvas. Bruce Tulloch was sent out with his company to undertake some fatigue work, and was fired upon by a Chinese battery. The company had to take cover until some Armstrong guns came up, but these were unable to silence the enemy's fire. Eventually a battery of smooth-bore nine-pounders had to come to their assistance, when the combined fire did eventually silence the Chinese guns.[11]

SOURCE NOTES

1 Hurd, D., *The Arrow War*, Collins, 1967.
2 Kenrick, N. C. E., *The Story of the Wiltshire Regiment*,Gale & Polden, 1963; Notebook of Captain P. S.Lumsden, National Army Museum.
3 Royal Archives, Windsor Castle, RA, VIC, ADD, MSS, E/1, 2894.
4 Wolseley, Lieut-Colonel G. J., *Narrative of the War with China in 1860*, Longman, Green, Longman & Roberts, 1862.
5 Atkinson, C. T., *Regimental History of the Royal Hampshire Regiment*, vol. 1, University Press, Glasgow, 1950.
6 Carter, T., *Historical Records of the 44th, or East Essex Regiment*, W. O. Mitchell, 1864.
7 Swinhoe, R., *Narrative of the North China Campaign of 1860*, Smith Elder, 1861.

8 Maxwell, E. L., *History of the 11th, King Edward's Own Lancers*, A. C. Curtis, 1914.

9 Hudson, Sir. H., *History of the 19th King George's Own Lancers, 1858–1924*, Gale & Polden, 1937.

10 Boyle, A. C., *History of Probyn's Horse*, Gale & Polden, 1929.

11 Bruce Tulloch, Sir A., *Recollections of Forty Years' Service*, Blackwood, 1903.

12 Bowlby, C. C., *An Account of the Last Mission and Death of Thomas William Bowlby*, private circulation, 1906.

13 Records of the King's Dragoon Guards, Regimental Museum of 1st The Queen's Dragoon Guards, Cardiff.

7

During the night of the 13th the Royal Engineers, with a working party drawn from the infantry regiments, managed to dig a trench to within 480 yards of the Chinese entrenchments at Tangku and with a frontage of some 200 yards, its right almost extending to the Pei-ho river. On the morning of 14 August the troops were ordered to march at 5.30 a.m. In view of de Montauban's fruitless foray towards Tangku after the storming of the Sinho entrenchment on the 12th, it was considered that the French had expended their turn to lead, and so the British were to have the place of honour in storming Tangku. The 1st Division would be in the lead, with the 2nd Division in reserve, occupying the 1st Division's old camping ground.

As the troops formed up, the British were on the right, close to the Pei-ho river, and the French were along the road. The artillery marched out with Barry's battery of Armstrong guns and Desborough's battery of nine-pounders taking up a position on the extreme right, while Milward's Armstrong guns and Govan's battery were positioned in the centre. Major Rigaud and 200 men of the 60th Rifles went forward in skirmishing order to protect the forward position of the guns. The Royal Scots and the 31st Regiment (East Surreys) followed the skirmishers, and The Queen's, the rest of the 60th Rifles, and the 15th Punjabis formed the second line.

As the advance progressed the troops came level with a hamlet on the opposite bank of the Pei-ho called Taleang-Tze, where the Chinese had moored two junks and constructed a small battery. The guns from the junks and the battery opened an annoying, though harmless, flank fire on the advancing infantry, so two Armstrong guns from Barry's battery were unlimbered and opened fire in order to silence them. Even though the range was only 250 yards, the Armstrong guns were not able to stop the Chinese bombardment. Some smooth bore guns from Desborough's battery were ordered up, and the combined fire managed to put an end to this nuisance. Some bluejackets from HMS *Chesapeake* followed up this success by crossing the Pei-ho in a commandeered junk, where they spiked two twelve-pounder and five six-pounder Chinese guns in the battery, and then set fire to the two junks. Whilst they were doing this, some Tartar cavalry appeared; the bluejackets fired at them with their pistols and then recrossed the Pei-ho to the British side. One sailor received a bullet through the arm.

By this time the French were in position with their left flank resting on the causeway leading to Tangku. The French had twelve guns forward and the British twenty-four, and all thirty-six came into action at about 800–900 yards' range. The Chinese replied with the fourteen guns which they had in the entrenchment, together with two guns positioned amongst some graves by the river. At the same time they maintained a heavy fire from the numerous gingals and matchlocks within the entrenchment. The walls were lined with flags, but as the Allied fire continued, these soon began to disappear. The skirmishers from the 60th Rifles moved forward and occupied the trench which had been dug the previous day by the Engineers' working party; from this cover they began to pick off the Chinese gunners. One of the Chinese mounted the wall of the entrenchment and stood there waving a flag, until a shot from one of the guns carried him away. The heavier weight of the Allied artillery soon began to tell, and the commander of the Royal Artillery moved his batteries forward by alternate bounds until the guns were firing from a range of only 450 yards. Soon the fire from the Chinese guns began to slacken, and then fell silent, although the gingals and matchlocks continued to shoot at the advancing infantry.[1,2]

Bruce Tulloch describes the advance of the infantry:

By some curious arrangement of the roster it fell to my fortunate lot to carry the Queen's colour. As we were advancing in line, I did not think the colours showed to proper advantage in their cases, and requested permission to display them properly. Floating out in the breeze in front of us as we advanced, they looked uncommonly well, and so thought a gun's crew in front of us, who within a minute afterwards sent a round-shot so close that the earth thrown up just brushed the colour party. Fortunately there happened to be a small gap in the line near to us, and the shot went through without doing any damage.[3]

Wolseley relates how

A party of the 60th Rifles, under Lieutenant Shaw, advanced to the extreme left flank of the entrenchment, which rested on the Pei-ho, where they managed to scramble across the ditch, and afterwards get behind the works.

Bruce Tulloch continues:

As we got close up to the work, I noticed a strip of firm ground between the ditch and the riverbank, and across this we went, and up onto the ramparts, displaying of course the colours to the best advantage on the top. The Regiment poured in and formed an irregular line, or rather obtuse angle, the Colonel – whose horse had been shot – and the colours at the apex. Nothing was left of the enemy at the corner, but the dead and dying gunners. The Chinese who were further along the wall, still steadily firing at the French, soon saw that the game was up, and rushed in a great crowd across the fort, and over the rear parapet. They went at such a pace that we could not get in with the bayonet, but we rapidly manned the rear parapet of the fort, and opened a tremendous fire on the fugitives. As usual when men are excited and begin fiddling with their sights in the old correct Hythe fashion, the fire was all too high, and the killed could be numbered on one's fingers.[1,3]

Whilst the British were forcing an entry, the French guns were continuing to fire for all they were worth, as the French, being forced to bridge the ditches in front of the entrenchment, had a more difficult task in gaining a footing. But soon the French tricolour appeared over the gateway.

Swinhoe was soon within the entrenchment:

Numbers of dead Chinese lay about the guns, some most fearfully lacerated. The wall afforded very little protection to the Tartar gunners, and it was astonishing how they managed to stand so long against the destructive fire that our Armstrongs poured upon them;

but I observed, in more instances than one, that the unfortunate creatures had been tied to the guns by the legs. Large baskets of powder, and shot of various sizes, lay near the guns, ready for use, with small flasks of finer powder, gun-pricks, and long coils of lighted fuse. The whole length of the wall mounted forty five pieces of artillery, of which sixteen were brass guns and the remainder iron. Dozens of bodies lay about the guns, dozens of others were found in the ditch that encircled the entrenchment, while numbers had crawled into the village to die, to say nothing of the scores that were carried down the river in junks, or conveyed away by the retreating force.

It was wonderful, notwithstanding the hot fire of the enemy, how little injury had been inflicted on our side. Not a single man was killed, only three English gunners were wounded and about a dozen French. General Michel had his horse killed under him.

Bruce Tulloch commented that

By custom of war the contents of a position carried by storm are the property of the captors, but as we left the fort, on return to our old camp, we noticed that as usual the non-combatants took possession of it. On this occasion they were led by a parson and a purveyor of the medical department, whom we saw rapidly overhauling the huts as we marched away.

As the 1st Division and the French returned to their camps, the 2nd Division, under Sir Robert Napier, was ordered into the entrenchment, and to occupy the village of Tangku.[3]

Grant reported on the action at Tangku:

Having arranged with General Montauban, we attacked the enemy's position on the 14th, and after a heavy fire of six batteries of artillery and three rocket batteries – two of the former French, and one of the latter – within 500 yards, we knocked their bastions to pieces and dismounted their guns. We got up so close to them with our artillery that they could not take aim, and I am happy to say in the whole attack we had only three men wounded, and the French one man killed and about twenty nine wounded. As the fire of the enemy began to slack, I passed the 60th Rifles down the side of the river through the reeds, at a part of the wall and ditch which the enemy had not made so strong, and they were enabled to get into the fort without much difficulty. I then sent to the French and told them what we had done, and they advanced and also got in. 16 excellent brass guns were taken in the fort, besides a number of iron ones. But, with the exception of one gun, they were of small calibre.[4]

When the Royal Scots got back to their camp, Bruce Tulloch found

my little package of personal baggage, which a brother officer, attached to the Coolie Corps, had found with that of other officers, lying on the Pehtang causeway. Not only the Regiment, but the Army, would have been in a bad way had it not been for that most valuable transport force, the Chinese Coolie Corps. The battalion of the Military Train, which came to China, were much digusted when they were told off to do the duty for which they had been created: the consequence was that the pack animals and native drivers, which the Military Train ought to have looked after, were utterly neglected; and a more disgraceful sight than the road from Pehtang, strewn with baggage, could not well be imagined.[3]

Grant needed several days in order to bring up supplies and to reconnoitre towards the Taku forts at the mouth of the Pei-ho river. The Commissariat also obtained as many supplies as they could from local sources, and on the afternoon of the 15th a number of Commissariat officers went out, escorted by some of the King's Dragoon Guards and some sowars, to buy sheep in a nearby village. As they neared the village they were fired upon by a Tartar cavalry picket. The KDG and Indians gave chase, killing three Tartars and wounding three others. All six were brought in with their horses and equipment; one of the wounded Tartars had been speared right through his body, and yet bore his sufferings with a stolid indifference.

The Taku forts now lay only some two miles in front of Tangku. Grant had determined to capture them; these bastions lying in his rear would otherwise provide a permanent threat to his communications, and a refuge from which the hordes of Tartar cavalry could attack his supplies as the main force made its way towards Peking. It would take several days both to bring up the heavy siege guns needed to reduce the forts and to establish a sufficient supply of ammunition, together with at least ten days' rations. A depot was immediately established at Sinho for this purpose.

There were four main Taku forts, two on each bank of the Pei-ho river. General de Montauban wanted, first, to cross the Pei-ho and attack the two southern forts, for he argued that by so doing it would enable the Navy to come up the Pei-ho and assist in the bombardment and assault of the two northern forts. Furthermore, by establishing themselves on the southern bank the Allies could effect the destruction of the Chinese forces opposing them, whereas if they remained on the north bank only, the Chinese would be left a means of retreat to Tientsin along the south bank of the Pei-ho. Grant, however, was more cautious and wanted time to think out the best method of attack. He wrote:

We are now in rear of the Pei-ho forts on the banks of the river, but the nature of the ground about there is anything but favourable to our advance. They are surrounded by great salt marshes, intersected with numerous large canals in every direction. We are now forming a bridge across the Pei-ho and trust to find the country there more adapted for the movements of an army. We have succeeded in procuring a sufficient number of junks, but I fear it will be several days before it can be got ready for crossing.[4]

Conditions between his base at Pehtang and Tangku added to Grant's difficulties. Although the weather was fine, with cool winds and cloudy days, an exceptionally high tide combining with a favourable wind on 16 August swamped part of the Pehtang causeway, submerging Grant's camp as well as that of the 1st Division. In addition there were comings and goings between the Allied camp and the Chinese, and a number of flags of truce passed to and fro. The Chinese arrived with the first flag of truce and with letters from the Governor General of Pechilli to Lord Elgin. Grant wrote that

The Governor General of Pechilli has sent in several letters praying Lord Elgin to put a stop to the war, and offering to take him up to Peking to settle a treaty. But Lord Elgin of course will not listen to this, and in his answer states that in consequence of the un-satisfactory reply to the demands of the British Minister conveyed in his letter of March last, the navy and military are engaged in taking possession of the Taku forts, and opening a passage for him to Tientsin.[4]

Accompanying the first Chinese flag of truce were two British soldiers who had been taken prisoner by the Chinese and were now being returned as a gesture of goodwill. It appeared that during the reconnaissance of 12 August a small party of the Chinese Coolie Corps, under an Irish sergeant of the 44th Regiment (Essex) and a private of The Buffs, No 2051 Private John Moyes, (often misspelt 'Moyse'), together with a Madras sapper, were in charge of some seventeen or eighteen Chinese of the Coolie Corps, engaged in bringing up rum to the troops of the 2nd Division. For whatever reason they fell far behind (Wolseley thought it was because they had broached the rum they were escorting), and then mistook a body of Tartar cavalry for Sikhs. After a scuffle they were taken prisoner and carried off to the Chinese camp.

On the following morning, the 13th, the whole party was brought before the Chinese General Sankolinsin, who ordered them to 'kowtow' to him. The kowtow was the traditional form of Chinese obeisance, and involved the subject falling down on his knees and bowing his head to the ground three times in front of the General. Sankolinsin promised that if the prisoners obeyed, no harm should come to them. It appears that the sergeant of the 44th and the Madras sapper, together with the Chinese coolies, obeyed the order and kowtowed. But Private Moyes of The Buffs, whether from effects of rum or because of natural courage, or perhaps because of sheer obstinacy, refused to kowtow. Sankolinsin then warned Moyes through an interpreter that if he continued to refuse, he would be beheaded by one of the escort. At this point Moyes declared that he would rather die than disgrace his country, whereupon he was at once beheaded and his corpse dragged away.

Bowlby, the *Times* correspondent, reported the incident, and it caught the eye of Sir Francis Doyle, who immortalised the event in a poem which paid full tribute to Moyes's courage, even if it lacked accuracy in all its details:

Last night among his fellow roughs
He jested, quaffed and swore,
A drunken private of the Buffs

73

Who never looked before.
Today beneath the foeman's frown
He stands in Elgin's place,
Ambassador from England's crown,
And type of all her race.

Far Kentish hopfields round him seemed
Like dreams to come and go,
Bright leagues of cherry blossom gleam'd
One sheet of living snow.
The smoke above his father's door
In soft grey eddies hung,
Must he then watch it rise no more,
Doomed by himself so young?

Yes, honour calls! with strength like steel
He puts the vision by;
Let dusky Indians whine and kneel,
An English lad must die.
And thus with eye that would not shrink,
With knee to man unbent,
Unfaltering on its dreadful brink,
To his red grave he went.

So let his name through Europe ring
A man of mean estate,
Who died, as firm as Sparta's king,
Because his soul was great.

The 'dusky Indians' were in fact Chinese coolies and
Moyes was himself a Scot, aged thirty-two, who had enlisted
at Edinburgh in 1845 and had been sent to The Buffs. The
Times report made no mention of the Irish sergeant of the 44th
nor of the Madras sapper. Whatever the inaccuracies, the
picture of a stalwart British private refusing to bow down to a
Chinese mandarin, and accepting death rather than disgrace
his regiment and his country, was greeted as a source of
inspiration.[5,6,7]

Neither Grant nor Wolseley were persuaded that Private
Moyes's action had been so heroic. Grant reported that

Two of our men, with several coolies, were taken prisoners as they
were conveying a cart with rum to the 2nd Division by the track
across the salt marsh. The mishap occurred owing to the carelessness

of the Europeans, who had not exerted themselves to keep up with the column.[7]

Wolseley was even more outspoken:

The first intimation we had of the circumstance was from one of these coolies who escaped that same night into Pehtang; and his story, which seems to be the correct one, was to the effect that the two soldiers drank rum until they became so intoxicated that they could not move, when shortly afterwards they were all taken prisoner. The Madras Sapper, overcome by hard work, and being unwell, had fallen out and laid down to sleep on the spot where he was captured. The soldier of the 44th who was sent in to us, either from the effects of bad treatment, or through a desire to screen his delinquencies, could not, or would not, give any connected account of his capture. His mind, indeed, seemed to be unbalanced, as in addition to the untruths he told, he talked utter nonsense about what he pretended he had overheard his captors say. His wrists bore traces of recent tying, and his hands were swollen from the tightness with which the cords had been fastened.

The captured coolies were also returned, having had their pigtails cut off by the Chinese, which was considered a great disgrace; but otherwise they had not been harmed, and instead of being treated as traitors by their countrymen, were sent back to the foreign invaders who had employed them.[1]

Grant, in writing to Sidney Herbert, was

most happy to inform you that the whole force is in excellent health, notwithstanding all the difficulties they have had to contend with. There is not above 1 per cent sick. The horses are also looking well and in excellent condition.

I am also happy to give you a good account of the Armstrong guns. Their precision of fire is admirable, and when the percussion shell explodes, nothing can be more effective, but I am sorry to say the damp seems to have affected them, and many appear useless. The time fuzes have also got injured in the same way, and have not been used . . .

[I have] reconnoitred the ground very closely on the left bank up to the northern fort. I found that by bridging several canals an approach could be got to it, and as it appeared to me it was the key of the position, I determined to attack it. I accordingly went to General Montauban and stated my proposition. The French General strongly objected. I told him, however, I was perfectly ready to undertake the attack myself if he did not wish to come. But he found it necessary to send a force to co-operate with me.[4]

Grant had come to the conclusion that if he could capture the northernmost fort nearest to Tangku, he could from there dominate by fire the three other forts; and events were subsequently to prove him right. In view of the prestige attaching to the French Army and its staff at that period, it required considerable strength of character on the part of Grant to override their views and to persist with the courage of his own convictions. De Montauban further protected his personal position by sending Grant a memorandum formally disagreeing with the decision Grant had taken.

Grant needed to build a bridge across the Pei-ho river, and a site was selected near Sinho, close to the camp of the 1st Division. However, the Chinese battery by the river, which had been silenced and had its guns spiked on the 14th, had now been re-established by the Chinese and was proving a nuisance to boats. Two Armstrong guns from Barry's battery were brought up and soon silenced the Chinese.

In order that national pride should be satisfied, it had been agreed that the bridge should be built half by the French and half by the British. The French won the toss, chose the south bank, and on 18 August Colonel Lévy of the French Engineers crossed the river with 300 men at a point where it was only 200 yards wide. As they landed on the other side they were fired upon by Chinese hiding in the orchards. The French soon drove these out, but in advancing further came upon an entrenchment defended by two to three hundred Chinese. The French stormed and took the entrenchment, but then found themselves surrounded by Tartar cavalry. General de Montauban sent infantry reinforcements across the river until the French force on the south bank numbered 1,000 men, and they were able to establish a secure bridgehead.

Some large flat-bottomed boats had been found in the various canals around Tangku, and these, together with some junks, formed the basis for a bridge of boats. Rope and timber were brought up from Pehtang, supplemented with material from Hong Kong. The greatest difficulty was in providing anchors for the boats – stone was in short supply – but a makeshift of wood fashioned to an Indian pattern, together with local millstones and captured Chinese roundshot, proved an adequate substitute. All the transport, including the artillery horses and waggons, was used to bring up materials, and the Coolie Corps provided much of the labour.

As soon as the bridge was completed General de Montauban marched 2,000 French across it to prove his point about the superiority of the southern approach. The French soon came to a halt because of the bad state of the roads on the southern side, and because it proved impossible to get forward without building a whole series of further bridges. Grant said nothing. Before long the French were back on the northern bank.

SOURCE NOTES

1 Wolseley, Lieut-Colonel G. J., *Narrative of the War with China, 1860*, Longman, Green, Longman & Roberts, 1862.
2 Swinhoe, R., *Narrative of the North China Campaign*, Smith Elder, 1861.
3 Bruce Tulloch, Sir Alexander, *Recollections of Forty Years' Service*, Blackwood, 1903.
4 Royal Archives, Windsor Castle, RA VIC ADD MSS E/1 2894.
5 Blaxland, G., *The Buffs*, Leo Cooper, 1972.
6 Selby, J., *The Paper Dragon*, Arthur Barker, 1968.
7 Knollys, H., *Incidents in the China War of 1860*, Blackwood, 1875.
8 Atkinson, C. T., *Regimental History of the Royal Hampshire Regiment*, vol. 1, University Press, Glasgow, 1950.

8

There were four Taku forts in all, two on each bank of the Pei-ho river; the two forts nearest the mouth of the river were the larger and principal forts, each with a smaller detached fort lying further up the river bank. It was the northernmost detached fort, which was only two miles from Tangku, that Grant intended to assault from behind, so avoiding the worst of any supporting fire from the other forts on the south bank. Once he had gained possession of this northernnmost fort, he was sure that he could dominate the three forts from their rear – though the Chinese reaction to this threat was to reverse the guns in the forts.

The northernmost fort was surrounded by a thick brick wall, suitably loopholed; immediately in front of the wall was, first of all, an open area embedded with sharpened stakes; in front of that again, a wide ditch full of water; then some twenty feet of open ground, thickly covered with pointed and sharpened bamboo stakes; then a second water-filled wide ditch; then another open space blocked by an abattis; and beyond this, finally, a deep dry ditch. All these obstacles had to be surmounted before the walls of the fort could be scaled. There was a causeway which led to the gate of the fort, and this crossed all the obstacles, but the bridge over the wet ditch nearest to the Allied troops had been destroyed, and the drawbridge over the other wet ditch, nearest the gate of the fort, had been raised.[1,2,3]

Grant had sent Captain Lumsden, of the Quartermaster General's staff of the 2nd Division, to carry out a reconnaissance of the way forward. The route chosen was now rapidly improved, under the superintendence of Major-General Sir Robert Napier who, as well as commanding the 2nd Division, was also one of the Army's best Engineer officers. On the night

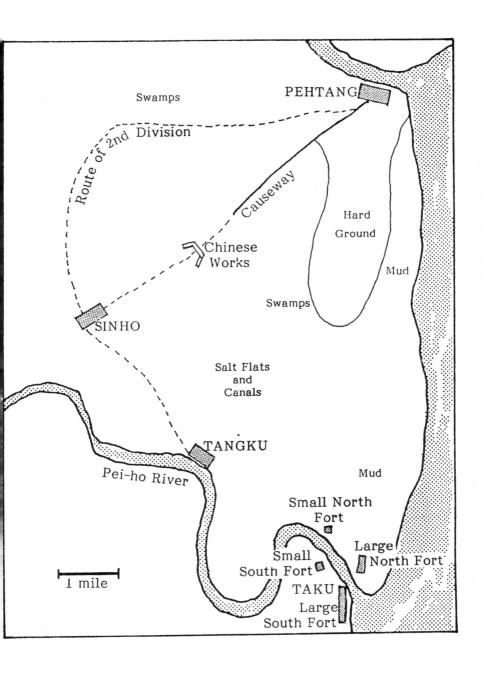

Swamps

PEHTANG

Route of 2nd Division

Causeway

Hard
Ground

Mud

Chinese
Works

Swamps

SINHO

Salt Flats
and
Canals

Mud

TANGKU

Pei-ho River

Small North
Fort

Large
North Fort

1 mile

Small
South Fort

TAKU

Large
South Fort

of 19 August pickets were pushed forward towards the northernmost Taku fort in order to protect the working parties provided by men of the 67th Regiment (Hampshires) under the supervision of the Royal Engineers.[2,4,5]

Grant gave orders that five batteries were to be built, and this work was carried out on the night of 20 August by means of two reliefs. Two of these battery positions were constructed with straw fascines, which had been found in the Tartar camps at Sinho and Tangku. On the following night the guns at Tangku were dismantled, brought forward and set up in the new positions ready for the coming assault. No. 1 Battery consisted of six French twenty-four-pounders and one British eight-inch gun; No. 2 Battery, whose gun platform was made from Chinese coffin lids, six inches thick, housed three British eight-inch mortars; No. 3 had two eight-inch mortars and two thirty-two-pounders, all British; No. 4 Battery had two eight-inch guns, and No. 5 Battery six Armstong guns, all British. These five main batteries were to bombard the detached northern fort to be assaulted, and in addition there were another nine guns positioned to fire at the forts on the southern banks of the Pei-ho. Finally, there were two Armstrong guns and two nine-pounders firing across the river at a Chinese entrenchment which threatened to enfilade the French right wing. Grant reported that on the night of the 20th bridges had been made over the canals, and batteries formed for heavy guns and mortars.[2,3,5,6]

It was also planned that four British gunboats, the *Clown*, *Drake*, *Janus* and *Woodcock*, together with four French gunboats, would cross the bar at the entrance of the Pei-ho river on the morning's tide, and that they would bombard the main fort on the north bank. Wolseley expressed some dissatisfaction that Admiral Hope did not send the gunboats up to the mouth of the Pei-ho earlier; in his opinion the Chinese would have had to respond to this threat and would have been unable to turn the guns of the forts to a landward direction; and so the attacking troops would have been saved from a heavier fire than was necessary. As the Chinese guns in the forts included two British thirty-two-pounders, which they had salvaged from the wrecks of the British gunboats sunk the year before and were now bringing into action against their previous owners, the feelings of the troops at the 'receiving end' were understandable.[2,3]

On 20 August Lord Elgin had despatched Mr Parkes and Major Graham of the Royal Engineers to the Taku forts, together with a guard from the 67th Regiment (Hampshires). The 67th halted some 1,000 yards from the northernmost fort, while Parkes and Graham approached it on their own, under a flag of truce. They asked to speak to the officer in charge, who eventually showed his head through an embrasure and asked their business. They said that they had come to offer terms of surrender, whereupon the mandarin grew abusive and told Parkes that if the Allies wanted the forts they had better come and take them. But then the Chinese tried to persuade Parkes that there should be a cessation of hostilities until such a time as the Imperial Commissioners should arrive from Peking. While this exchange was going on, Major Graham noted the layout and strength of the fort. As the party returned to their lines, the guns of both the northern forts opened fire on the 67th's working parties. Milward's battery of Armstrong guns, which was up in support, returned the fire, but little damage had been done except for some near misses to the men of the 67th and the destruction of some of their camp kettles. Lord Elgin decided that the idea of a temporary truce was merely a delaying tactic on the part of the Chinese, and so the offer was ignored.[2,3,4,5]

During the night of 20 August the Chinese kept up an intermittent fire from the guns of the forts, but did little damage. They were clearly nervous, and from time to time fired a number of fireballs to illuminate the scene. These had a disconcerting effect on some of the young recruits of the 67th, who lay down and then took some time to get onto their feet again once the fireball had burnt itself out.[2,4]

At daybreak, which was at five o'clock, the Chinese guns from the forts opened fire, an hour before the Allies intended to start their bombardment. As a result the Allied batteries opened fire in return earlier than planned, and at six o'clock a lucky shot exploded a magazine within the northernmost fort. Wolseley described the scene:

At about six o'clock in the morning when the fire waxed hotter and hotter, everyone being intent upon the scene then before him, and all anxiously speculating as to when the signal for a general advance would be given, a tall black pillar, as if by magic, shot up from the midst of the nearest fort upon which almost all our fire was concentrated, and then bursting like a rocket after it had attained a great height, was soon lost in the vast shower of wood and earth into which it resolved itself, – a loud, bursting, booming sound, marking, as it were, the moment of its short existence. A magazine had blown up.

The fire from the Chinese guns then ceased, and some of the British officers watching considered that the forthcoming attack would be easy. It was not long, however, before the guns of the fort re-opened fire. Wolseley commented: 'As long as a gun was left them they were determined to serve it, and most manfully they did so, all the while exposed to a most crushing shell fire brought to bear upon them, and with but little, and in some instances, no protection whatever against it.'[2,3,6]

Half an hour later there was a second and similar explosion in the main fort on the north bank. This was generally attributed to the fire from the gunboats at the mouth of the Pei-ho, although the Armstrong gunners also claimed the credit. Wolseley was critical of the Navy's performance, as only two British and two French gunboats managed to get within sufficient range of the lower forts without coming themselves within reach of the heavy guns of these forts, and as a result the effect of their fire could not be accurately observed.[2,6]

Whilst the bombardment continued, the attacking troops were brought up from their camps, near Tangku. The French took the right flank, the British attacked on the left, which was the side most exposed to the fire from the main fort of the northern bank. The storming party consisted of a wing of the 44th (Essex) under command of Lieutenant-Colonel Patrick MacMahon, and a wing of the 67th under Lieutenant-Colonel

Thomas. The storming party was supported by the other wings of the 44th and 67th, and by the Royal Marines under Lieutenant-Colonel Gascoigne. Another detachment of Royal Marines, under Lieutenant-Colonel Travers, carried a pontoon bridge to be used in crossing the wet ditches, the placing of which was to be under the supervision of a party of Royal Engineers commanded by Lieutenant Pritchard, RE. Three other parties of Royal Engineers carried scaling ladders, powder bags and the means to remove other obstacles, all the Engineers being commanded by Major Graham, RE. The whole British assaulting force was commanded by Brigadier-General Reeves and numbered some 1,500 men. The French force left Tangku some time after the British and was made up of about 1,000 infantry and six twelve-pounder rifled guns. It was commanded by General Collineau.[4,5,7]

Grant, reporting on this part of the action, wrote:

I took 1,500 men of the 2nd Division under Major-General Sir Robert Napier – 2 Armstrong batteries – and four 24 pounder howitzers. The French sent General Collineau with 1,000 men and two batteries. And on the morning of the 21st, the troops and guns being in position, the enemy from the fort and the batteries on the other side of the river opened a heavy fire, which, however, annoyed us little, and they were soon answered by our guns, which fired with great precision, and a mortar shell fell into their magazine and exploded it. The English and French gunboats now commenced a heavy fire upon the lower north fort, and also exploded one of their large magazines. The effect of these two going off was magnificent, and it was supposed the enemy would have evacuated the forts immediately after. I, however, never saw a stouter resistance.[6]

By seven o'clock every Chinese gun in the detached northern fort had been dismounted or silenced. Two batteries of field guns were then pushed forward to within 500 yards of the fort, and at the same time some companies of the 44th and 67th advanced to within thirty yards of the fort in order to open up a covering fire of close-quarter musketry on the defenders lining the walls. This forced the guns to lower their rate of fire for fear of hitting their own troops, and this in turn encouraged the Chinese to man the walls, from where they opened a heavy fire of musketry on the attackers.[2,4,5,7]

After the skirmishers the British advance was led by the pontoon-carrying parties, which made the best speed they could along the narrow causeway straight towards the main gates at the rear of the fort. At the same time the French advanced towards the angle of the fort which abutted onto the river. Here the two ditches terminated some way from the river bank, and some of the French, seeing this, managed to get around the end of the first ditch. Others had thrown ladders across and managed to scramble them. These ladders had been carried into action for the French by their Chinese coolies, and Wolseley remarked, 'I have never seen men under fire behave with greater coolness, or perform their allotted work in a more manner-of-fact way.' Swinhoe relates how they stood 'up to their necks in the ditches holding ladders over their heads to enable the men to cross'. Some of the French then got across the second wet ditch and tried to scale the walls of the fort, but were halted by the strength of the resistance from the Chinese lining the walls.[2,3]

The British were not so fortunate, for the pontoon parties were proving more of a hindrance than a help. As men carrying the unwieldy pontoons were wounded, frequent halts had to be made; then a round shot hit one of the pontoons, rendering it useless and causing fifteen casualties. The causeway became blocked and the Marines and Engineers, continuing their unsuccessful attempts to bridge the ditch, suffered further casualties. The advancing infantry of the 44th and 67th were all the time subjected to a tremendous fire from the defending Chinese; now, without waiting any longer for the ditches to be bridged, the men plunged into the mud and water, which came up to their armpits, and swam or struggled across to the other side. On clambering out of the ditches they were faced with the sharpened bamboo stakes, through which they smashed their way and then broke down the abattis until they reached the foot of the wall. Others ran along the ditches looking for a possible crossing place. Meanwhile musketry, pots filled with lime, round shot, arrows, crossbow bolts, and bunches of slugs fired from gingals showered down on the attackers, and men were being killed and wounded, until the small area was covered with the dead and dying.[2,4,5,7]

Sir Robert Napier, seeing the confusion, brought up two howitzers of Captain Govan's battery to within fifty yards of the main gate of the fort, and these soon managed to create a small breach by the main gate. Some of the more determined spirits had reached the main gate, and a corporal of the 67th produced an axe. Wolseley describes how

Colonel Mann, of the Royal Engineers, who was amongst the first over the two ditches, with Major Anson, ADC, had, after much hacking and cutting with their swords, succeeded in severing the ropes which held up the drawbridge. Down it came with a crash, but it was so shattered by shot that, at first, it seemed incapable of sustaining any weight. A single beam of the outer bridge had been left by the Chinese; it was quite loose and rolled about, yet it enabled many to cross over. The quaint joking of our men was most amusing whenever any unlucky fellow, whilst crossing, overbalanced himself and fell into the ditch, from whence he climbed up the muddy bank opposite, there perchance to meet his deathblow, ere the very smile at his own mishap had passed from his countenance.[2,4]

In the meantime some of the supporting headquarters wing of the 67th, under Colonel Knox, had crossed the ditches by the ladders put in place by the French, and others had swum across. By now a group of officers and men had assembled by the main gate, where the guns of Govan's battery had effected the small breach, through which it was almost possible to pass in single file. Lieutenant Burslem, helped by Private Lane, both of the 67th, managed to enlarge the breach and squeezed through into the fort. Burslem was thrust back by the Chinese defenders, but he and Lane pushed their way forward a second time. As they did so, Burslem and Lane were both severely wounded, but they had forced a way into the fort. For their gallantry they were both awarded the Victoria Cross.[2,4]

Just before this, Lieutenant Rogers, commanding the leading 'E' Company of the 44th, together with Private McDougall of the same regiment, was helped by Lieutenant Lenon of the

67th, who forced his sword and some bayonets into the mud of the wall of the fort. Rogers climbed up them and gained an entrance through an embrasure. Officially credited with being the first within the fort, he was awarded the Victoria Cross, as were Private McDougall of the 44th (Essex) and Lieutenant Lenon of the 67th (Hampshires)[4,7,11]

When Lieutenant Chaplin, carrying the Queen's Colour of the 67th, reached the wall, he climbed up on the backs of some of his men and was then pushed and pulled by them until he scrambled onto the parapet of the fort, where he was joined by Private Lane of the 67th from the breach. Backed by more men of the 67th, who had now managed to join him on the parapet, Chaplin and his party advanced up a ramp, using their bayonets to good effect on the Chinese defenders. Chaplin then planted the Queen's Colour on the cavalier for all to see. For his gallantry and leadership, which cost him three severe wounds, he was awarded the Victoria Cross. Thus six Victoria Crosses were won at Taku by the officers and men of the 44th (Essex) and the 67th (Hampshire) for their outstanding courage.[2,4]

On the right flank the French had also been attempting to scale the wall. Placing their ladders against the wall, the French infantry began to climb up, but the Chinese defenders threw back the ladders with the men on them. After several brave attempts, one Frenchman, carrying a tricolour, jumped from his ladder onto the parapet, waving the tricolour amidst wild cheers from his companions, but at once fell shot through the heart. Inspired by his example, others forced their way onto the parapet and were able to enter the fort just before the British.[2,3]

With both the British and French troops now inside the fort the fighting became even fiercer, for the Chinese were hampered by their own defences and unable to escape easily. It was their turn now to cross the ditches and the sharpened bamboo stakes, and their only means of flight was over the wall facing the river, where the defences were at their strongest. They were cleared from the fort by a combination of the bayonet and Captain Govan's guns, which had been moved to a position where by firing canister they caught the Chinese as they were driven over the walls. Grant reported that 'The ground outside the fort was literally strewn with the enemy's dead and wounded. Three of the Chinese were impaled on the stakes.' Some tried to hold out in huts and in the corners of the fort, but they were soon 'mopped up'. One of the Chinese generals had been killed in the bombardment, and a second, who was in command of both the northern forts, and a 'red button Mandarin' of the highest rank, refused to surrender and fought to the last, finally being shot by an officer of the Royal Marines during the fighting inside the fort. Brigadier Reeves, commanding the British assault, was himself wounded more than once, but refused to leave the field until he saw that the fort had been taken. [2,3,4,6,7]

The scene inside the fort reflected the savagery of the bombardment and of the subsequent assault. Wolseley entered the fort and saw that 'our artillery had done its part, and the debris caused by the explosion of the magazine lay in heaps everywhere, intermingled with overturned cannon, broken gun-carriages, and the dead and wounded of the garrison'. The force was accompanied by Signor Beato, an Italian photographer from Calcutta, who set up his apparatus, refusing to allow bodies to be moved until he had recorded the grim scene for posterity. His photographs of the China Campaign of 1860 must rank, along with those of Fenton's of the Crimea, among the most interesting early photographic records of war. [2]

Captain Hart Dunne of the 99th (Wiltshires) had managed to get himself a staff appointment away from his regiment, which had been left to garrison Pehtang. Hart Dunne climbed a flagpole in the captured fort and hoisted a Union Jack at the masthead, but while he was thus engaged, a French soldier quietly stole his brandy flask. [8]

Grant, reporting on this phase of the action, wrote:

When our troops – English and French – got up to the walls with their scaling ladders, they [the Chinese] fought most desperately with pikes and lances, and struck down many a brave fellow. Our men were, however, not to be kept back, and they got over at two parts of the wall. The poor Chinese had little hope of escape. Two deep ditches ran round the walls, and between them an abattis, and two broad rows of pointed bamboo stakes, which it was nearly impossible to get over. Two Tartar generals were killed and a number of their men. The fort being in our possession, we had complete command of the highest on the other side of the river.[6]

Grant now brought up the heavy guns, some of which were unlimbered and set in position to the left of the fort, ready to open fire on the main fort on the north bank, whilst others were put into place on the raised cavalier inside the captured fort. The range between the two forts on the north bank was exactly 1,000 yards, and there was a raised causeway between them. The ground between the causeway and the Pei-ho was of soft mud, but on the other northern side the going was firm. The Buffs and the 8th Punjabis were brought forward ready to attack the main fort, and a reconnaissance party went out to look at the route to be taken. This small party, under command of an officer of the Quartermaster General's department, came under a heavy fire from the three Chinese forts as they advanced cautiously in skirmishing order.[1,2,3,4,9,10]

Suddenly a white flag was hoisted on the main fort on the south bank, followed by more white flags from the other two forts, and the Chinese ceased firing. Then a messenger appeared from the main north fort carrying a flag of truce. Parkes went forward to meet this envoy, who turned out to be General Sankolinsin's interpreter of English, whom Swinhoe described as 'an impudent native of Shanghai, who had formerly acted as linguist in an American firm at that place'. He brought with him a letter, addressed to Lord Elgin and Baron Gros, which stated that as the Allies had captured one fort, the Chinese would now remove the booms from the river and allow the Allies safe conduct to Tientsin, where peace terms could be agreed. This was considered to be an insulting response, and so the letter was crumpled up and thrown back at the messenger. He was told that unless the remaining forts surrendered before two o'clock, the next fort would be stormed and taken.[1,2,3]

At two o'clock the sky had become overcast when the British and the French began to advance. There was no resistance from the Chinese; not a shot was fired as the troops advanced on the main north fort. The French dashed on ahead of The Buffs and Punjabis and, scaling the walls, entered by an embrasure, to find within the fort some 2,000 Chinese soldiers crowded together. The Buffs soon rounded up all the Chinese within the fort. The Tartars had thrown away their weapons and their military caps and were expecting on capture to be executed. When they were told that they could all leave, they had difficulty in understanding that they were free. At this point the threatened storm broke and the rain came down in torrents.[1,2,3,9]

Grant reported:

As white flags were immediately hoisted upon all the other forts, we sent a flag of truce to summon them to surrender. The enemy however stated that they had no order on the subject, and we proceeded to attack the lower fort on the north side. Not a shot was fired by the enemy, and we entered without any opposition. Upwards of 2,000 prisoners were taken, and numerous fine large brass guns, also several of the large guns which had been taken out of the gunboats in '59. The white flags still continued flying on the other forts, and as the garrison were seen marching out of the large southern one, I sent a party in conjunction with the French to occupy it, and our two flags are now flying from the summit of the highest bastion. Immediately I sent Mr Parkes over, who has proved himself a most useful interpreter and has on all occasions displayed the greatest zeal and utility, to confer with the Governor General, who agreed to surrender unconditionally the whole of the guns, forts, camps and munitions of war about the forts.[6]

When the Chinese were seen to be evacuating the large southern fort, Hope Grant had a mixed party of some 300 of The Buffs and French infantry ferried across the Pei-ho in ships' boats. Both parties raced for the fort, with The Buffs just managing to hoist a Union Jack on the ramparts before the French planted their tricolour. So ended an eventful day.[2,9]

SOURCE NOTES

1 Fortescue, Hon. J. W., *History of the Army*, vol.13, chapter 55, Macmillan, 1917.

2 Wolseley, Lieut-Colonel G. J., *Narrative of the War with China in 1860*, Longman, Green, Longman & Roberts, 1862.

3 Swinhoe, R., *Narrative of the North China Campaign*, Smith Elder, 1861.

4 Atkinson, C. T.,*Regimental History of the Royal Hampshire Regiment*, vol.1, University Press, Glasgow, 1950.

5 Porter, Major-General, W., *The History of the Corps of Royal Engineers*, vol.1, 1889.

6 Royal Archives, Windsor Castle, RA, VIC, ADD, MSS, E/1, 2894.

7 Carter, T., *Historical Records of the 44th or East Essex Regiment*, W. O. Mitchell, 1864.

8 Kenrick, N. C. E., *The Story of the Wiltshire Regiment*, Gale & Polden, 1963.

9 Blaxford, G., *The Buffs*, Leo Cooper, 1972.

10 *Historical Records of the 20th Infantry (Duke of Cambridge's Own)*, *Brownlow's Punjabis*, Swiss & Co., 1909.

11 Burrows, J., *The Essex Regiment*, J. Burrows, 1938.

9

The capture of the Taku forts had been achieved, but at a comparatively heavy cost. Grant reported, 'I regret to say our loss has been comparatively heavy – 17 men killed, 19 Officers and about 153 men wounded. The French loss is, I believe, about 100.' A later count put the British casualties at 201, and the French at 158. The two regiments which had borne the brunt of the assault were the 44th (Essex) and the 67th (Hampshires). The 44th had Captain Ingham and Lieutenant Rogers severely wounded, with fourteen men killed and one drummer and forty-five men wounded. The 67th had eight officers wounded, Lieutenant-Colonel Thomas, Captain Miller, Lieutenants Burslem, Kingsley and Lenon, and Ensigns Chaplin, Fraser and Turner. Six men of the 67th were killed, and sixty-three wounded, of whom four later died of their wounds. The Royal Engineers under Major Graham, RE, who was himself wounded, together with the pontoon-carrying party of the Royal Marines, also suffered heavy casualties.[1,2,3,4]

Swinhoe remembered that

It was a sorrowful sight to pass the litters bringing back the wounded, each carried by two coolies. Everyone felt anxious as they passed to know what friend or comrade was inside them. Our poor fellows, though often in great pain, were cheerful when they witnessed the prompt manner in which their comforts were attended to.[5]

The Medical Department had made excellent arrangements for the campaign; regimental hospitals were done away with, and all medical officers were placed under the disposal of the Principal Medical Officer, William Muir, so that he could concentrate them at the point where they were most needed. Following the criticisms of the hospital services in the Crimea, some forty medical officers and a large contingent of the Army Hospital Corps had been ordered to accompany the force. The result of such arrangements became clear at the storming of the Taku forts, for all the casualties were dealt with so speedily that the men were given great confidence. And this trust was reinforced by the courage of the Chinese coolies, six of whom were wounded in tending the casualties and in carrying them out of action.

Regimental dressing stations had been set up at Tangku, some two and a half miles from the scene of the action, and it was to these that the wounded were carried in the first instance. From there, after immediate treatment, they were passed on, by means of litters slung between ponies, to the two hospital ships which lay off Pehtang. Each ship had 200 beds and was equipped with operating theatres, and every casualty was aboard within thirty-six hours of being wounded; most of the necessary operations had been performed by then. In addition to the two hospital ships, a transport and a sailing ship had been set aside for the use of the British sick, and four more ships for the Indian casualties. Within eight days following the action at Taku, some 200 sick, including some cholera cases, were evacuated to the ships.[6]

The bodies of the Chinese dead lay everywhere, both inside and outside the forts; their wounded, mainly northern Chinese, Mongols and Manchurians, were carried to a hut within the main fort on the south bank of the Pei-ho, from whence they were removed to Tangku once the Allied wounded were safely aboard the hospital ships. In this Chinese hospital there was a boy with nine bayonet wounds; he was a cake-seller who had gone into the fort the night before the attack in order to sell his wares, and had then not been allowed to leave. As the Allied troops stormed in he hid under a mat and was bayoneted again and again as the soldiers searched the place for fugitives. Eventually he was hauled out and to his surprise, instead of being despatched on the spot, was taken care of and had his wounds treated.[5,6]

The torrential rain which had fallen just as the forts were captured made the ground impassable. Grant commented that

'Half an hour after the attack was completed, it commenced to rain very heavily, and our heavy guns could not be moved.' Wolseley was more explicit:

The road by which we advanced to the forts was for a considerable distance quite submerged, and the uncovered spots were so deep with mud that even the very lightest of our guns were only dragged through it by the united exertions of long teams of horses, aided by the tired gunners themselves, who kept spoking away at the wheels. No amount of horses, and of men attached to drag-ropes, could move our heavy guns or waggons; their wheels sank deeper and deeper every minute, until their naves touched the mud.[1,7]

That night was a miserable one for the soldiers, after they had dragged themselves the five miles back to their camps around Tangku and Sinho in the pouring rain. The camps were flooded and firewood was so wet that it was impossible to light any fires; so for the majority, who had not eaten all day, there were only ration biscuits to supplement whatever else they could themselves provide.

It seemed to Grant that with the capture of the Taku forts, the opening up of the Pei-ho river, and the signing of the Terms of Capitulation, the campaign must be at an end. He wrote, 'I trust that the war is nearly, if not completely, at an end.' Wolseley wrote home from Taku: 'The war is over.' These hopes were soon to be disillusioned.[1,7]

Admiral Hope and the Royal Navy now went about the clearance of the obstacles blocking the entrance to the Pei-ho river. The morning after the capture of the forts the gunboats crossed the bar and started to remove the booms and stakes which covered the entrance to the river. The first obstacle was a row of iron stakes, each weighing several tons with one end embedded in the mud of the river bottom. There then followed a boom across the river, which was supported by earthen jars to give it buoyancy. The third obstruction was another row of iron stakes, then a line of boats filled with incendiary material, and finally a second boom. The gunboats did not take long to clear sufficient of these obstacles to enable them to open a channel, and as soon as this was done,

Admiral Hope entered the river. The hulks of the British gunboats *Plover* and *Lee*, sunk in 1859, were still visible at low tide.[5,7]

The next day, 23 August, Admiral Hope in the *Coromandel*, escorted by five gunboats, made his way up river. The Chinese did not attempt to oppose the advance and the forts at Shwang-cheang were found to be deserted, allowing the small squadron of boats to anchor some ten miles below Tientsin that evening. A group of Chinese merchants from Tientsin approached Admiral Hope and told him that, in spite of considerable defences having been thrown up around the city, the Imperial troops had retreated towards Peking. General Sankolinsin had ridden past the city, without entering it, on the evening of the 22nd, together with a small band of soldiers. By this time the British soldiers had invented a story that General Sankolinsin was in reality a renegade Irish deserter from the Royal Marines, whose real name was Sam Collinson; and thereafter the Chinese Commander was known to all the men as 'Sammy Collinson'.

Grant at the Taku forts was able to report on the 24th that

I have just heard from Admiral Hope that he had got up within a short distance of Tientsin, and that the forts had been all abandoned. A Mandarin and deputation came out from the town, and tendered their submission.[1]

On the morning of 24 August the squadron moved up to Tientsin, landing small parties of Royal Marines to occupy each of the abandoned forts guarding the city. A further party of Royal Marines seized the eastern gate of Tientsin, and unfurled a Union Jack and a tricolour from the top. The Chinese Viceroy and two of the Imperial Commissioners, who had been sent by the Emperor to escort Lord Elgin to Peking, visited Admiral Hope on board the *Coromandel*, where they were informed that the Allies had taken possession of Tientsin but that the local authorities would be allowed to continue to function as normal. Mr Parkes, the Consular Officer from Canton, interviewed the mandarins of the city and arranged for some of the local merchants, who had been responsible for

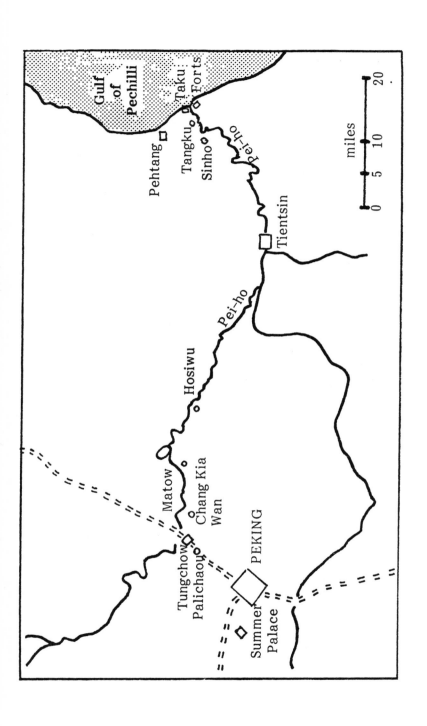

Gulf
of
Pechilli

Taku Forts

Tangku
Sinho

Pehtang

Pei-ho

Tientsin

Pei-ho

Hosiwu

Matow

Chang Kia
Wan

Tungchow
Palichiao

PEKING

Summer
Palace

miles

0   5   10   20

feeding the Imperial Chinese forces, to supply the Allied troops as they arrived.

Grant decided to move the main part of the force up to Tientsin. There were two roads, one along each bank of the Pei-ho river, and there was the river itself. Grant and Elgin, together with the 1st Royal Scots, the 67th (Hampshires) and a battery of the Royal Artillery, were loaded into gunboats and travelled up the river to Tientsin, leaving Taku on 25 August. The Royal Scots' passage was not as smooth as it might have been. Bruce Tulloch recalled that

We, 500 in number, were placed on board the *Bustard*: there was only standing room, and away we went up the river to have a go at the river forts guarding Tientsin. Unfortunately, just as it got dusk, we grounded, and notwithstanding the employment of every nautical device, we had to remain hard and fast until the tide rose. Standing up all night was not pleasant, but there was not even room for the senior officers to ease their legs. It was not long after daybreak that we got within sight of the forts, massively constructed, like those at Taku, and with heavy guns in them. The disgust of the regiment may be imagined when we found we should not have a chance of distinguishing ourselves. The Chinese for the time being had had enough of it, and on our approach abandoned the forts.[5,7,8]

The Cavalry Brigade also set out for Tientsin from their camp at Sinho on 25 August. They marched along the north bank of the Pei-ho through open flat country, dotted with orchards near to the river, and reached Tientsin on the 27th, crossing over the Pei-ho into the city by a bridge of boats. They encamped on the flat and open ground around the city.

The Buffs were left at Taku to garrison the forts and to guard the entrance to the river, whilst the 60th Rifles remained at the camps at Sinho to protect the bridge of boats and the lines of communication. News had reached the force that the Taiping rebels were threatening Shanghai, and the 44th (Essex) were ordered on 25 August, at a few hours' notice, to embark for that port, where they remained until 15 November. As a result of these dispositions the strength of Grant's force was reduced by three infantry battalions, but as the general feeling was that the war was over bar the shouting, this was not considered to be of too much significance. Indeed Grant was thinking of sending back the 1st Royal Scots to Britain.

The main body of the army set out from Taku to march for Tientsin, with the 1st Division leading up the right bank of the Pei-ho, and the 2nd Division following; the French contingent used the road to the north or left bank of the river. The troops had to move off by detachments owing to the boggy state of the ground and the difficulty in finding any firm place to camp for the night. Because of this the battery of the Royal Artillery had to stay on the roadway overnight; surrounding ground was marshy and there was a deep ditch running alongside the road. As the troops neared Tientsin the country became more open and firm. The leading troops of the 1st Division reached the city on 1 September, but the 99th (Wiltshires), who had up to then been the garrison battalion at Pehtang, did not leave the area of Pehtang and Sinho until the beginning of September, and they, like Brownlow's Punjabis, who set out on 31 August, did not arrive at Tientsin until 5 September.

Swinhoe watched the 99th leave:

As I wandered along I heard the loud uniform footfall of a regiment marching over wooden boards, and, looking to the bridge of boats, observed the red coats of the 99th. They had come all the way from Pehtang that day in order to join our march [that of the 2nd Division]. The men were much fagged and required a day's rest after their long tramp.

He then goes on to describe a typical day's march:

At four o'clock next morning, the bugle sounded the Reveille; tents were struck and in an hour we were on the march. We passed through [villages and] a halt was called, while the advance officers rode on to headquarters to receive orders about the encamping ground. This occasioned a most tedious delay, of two hours duration, in the hot sun. Everyone was nearly driven crazy. At last the advance bugle sounded, and we went on, till the large grassy plain in front of the walls of Tientsin opened to view, with the distant gathering of tents of the advance army. The bands of our division struck up in high glee, and we soon sought refuge from the sun's burning glare, lying prostrate in our tents.[5]

Elgin and Grant set up their headquarters in the house of the Salt Commissioner, which lay close enough to the river for boats coming up to the city to be able to tie up a few yards from the doorway. The house was the property of Tsung Han, a member of the wealthy Han family of Tientsin, and was sufficiently large to accommodate Baron Gros, so that both the British and the French diplomatic embassies and the Commander-in-Chief were all together. General de Montauban occupied a joss-house nearby.

The three Imperial Commissioners arrived at Tientsin from Peking on 31 August, and after protracted negotiations it was agreed that a Convention should be signed on 7 September. On 6 September Parkes and Mr Thomas Wade met with the Commissioners to arrange the details for the signing on the following day. At this point Parkes discovered that none of the Imperial Commissioners had any authority to sign. It then became clear that the negotiations had merely been a delaying tactic or, worse still, an attempt to entice Lord Elgin to proceed to Peking with only a small escort and so be at the mercy of the Imperial authorities. This was later confirmed when official papers, which were subsequently captured in the Imperial Palace at Peking, made it clear that the purpose of the negotiations was to gain time in the hope of extending the operations until the cold weather brought all military operations to a standstill. The fact that Elgin had been prepared to go to Peking with only a small escort was made evident by Bowlby, the *Times* correspondent, who noted on 4 September that he had

Received [an] invitation from Lord Elgin to go to Peking. We only take up to 1,000 men, of whom it is arranged that the KDG's shall form 300, Probyn gives 100, Fane 100, and fifty picked men from each Regiment, with a Battery.[9]

With the collapse of the negotiations Elgin at once instructed Grant to continue the advance on Peking, and the Imperial Commissioners were told that no further meetings would be arranged until they produced the Imperial Decree authorising them to sign the Convention. A week had been wasted and the troops, who had accepted without question the assurances of the negotiators that the war was over, had now to prepare themselves for more fighting. The 1st Foot, The Royal Scots, who, having served in the garrison in Hong Kong for several years before the expedition, and whose numbers were in consequence very much reduced, thought that they were about to return to Britain, and some of the officers, in anticipation, had sold off their heavy baggage and animals by public auction. A more serious result was that on the night of 9 September all the local Chinese drivers with their carts, mules and ponies, which had been collected with great difficulty during the time spent at Tientsin, suddenly disappeared, taking advantage of a thunderstorm to make their escape without being noticed. Grant reported to the Duke of Cambridge:

It was my intention to send back to England the 1st Royals and Rotton's Battery, supposing that the war was nearly at an end. By the official letters sent you will perceive that the Chinese have acted with bad faith.[10]

The delay caused by the fruitless negotiations had at least enabled Grant to concentrate his force at Tientsin, and had given the troops a short period of rest before the next stage of the campaign. The regiments were encamped on the grassy plain around Tientsin and the Medical Services had taken over a large temple in the city as a hospital, which made seventy beds available for the use of both officers and men. This was to act as a casualty clearing station, with the sick and wounded being evacuated as soon as possible on small steamers down the Pei-ho to the hospital ships lying off the mouth of the river. The weather was warm, with temperatures reaching 100 degrees, but the nights remained cool and fresh and the number of men falling sick remained low.[6]

During the first few days at Tientsin the troops were sheltered in issue British Army bell tents, which seemed to capture all the heat and imprison it, but very shortly Indian tents which were much larger and more airy came up from

Pehtang. The Chinese established a good market close to the camp, where tea, mutton and beef were readily available, fresh fruit and vegetables were plentiful, as were, most appreciated of all, large quantities of ice. As Lord Elgin commented, 'A man scorns his grog if it is not well iced.'

It was as well that local supplies were plentiful for the Military Train continued to draw a great deal of adverse comment. Bowlby, witnessing their performance at first hand, joined the criticism:

The Military Train, on its march here, lost one day's rations for 1,500 men. Supposed that the animals fell down and their loads left behind. These gentlemen are above this work and the Corps wants reorganising. I saw plenty of fallen animals on the line of march but in no case did I see an MT descend to assist them. They sit on their horses while the drivers lick the poor worn out ponies, never dreaming of aiding them to rise by relieving their load. The junks arrived tonight with six days provisions for the force. Good work. They were only sent for on Tuesday.[9]

It was fortunate the troops were not solely dependent on land-borne transport.

The Chinese willingness to bring into market plentiful supplies was helped by the strict discipline enforced by Grant, who severely punished any cases of looting. Now that the army was concentrated forward at Tientsin and because supplies were easily obtainable, both from local sources and up the Pei-ho, Grant decided to close down the base at Odin Bay. The 19th Punjabis and the few men of the Royal Artillery left to guard the Commissariat Depot at Odin Bay were ordered to join the main force.

Owing to the acute shortage of transport, resulting from the defection of the locally recruited Chinese and their mules and carts, Grant decided to move forward towards Tungchow by detachments. The 2nd Division was to be left at Tientsin, under Sir Robert Napier, but was to be ready to advance in support of the 1st Division as soon as its services were required. The first detachment to advance, under command of Brigadier-General Reeves, was made up of the King's Dragoon Guards and Fane's Horse, of the Cavalry Brigade;

with the 99th Regiment (Wiltshires) and 200 Royal Marines providing the infantry; and with Barry's and Stirling's batteries of the Royal Artillery in support. This advance guard was to set out on 8 September and would also provide a bodyguard for Lord Elgin. The second detachment was to be 3,000 of the French contingent, who would leave Tientsin on 10 September. Sir John Michel, commanding the 1st Division, would then advance with the 2nd Brigade on 12 September, together with Probyn's Horse and Desborough's battery of the Royal Artillery. The siege train would be brought up by the river, together with as many supplies as possible, but it was feared that the Pei-ho might only be navigable as far as Hosiwu, which was only a little more than half of the sixty miles to Tungchow; and Tungchow itself was still twenty miles from Peking.

Swinhoe watched the departure of the first detachment:

Next day [the 7th] Sir Hope Grant pushed out an advance guard on the road to Tungchow, and encamped them some miles beyond Tientsin, at the same time giving orders that the march should commence the following day. Accordingly, on the morning of the 8th, I was roused from my slumbers by the band of the Rifles [60th] playing 'Old Folks at Home', and, turning out, saw that the march had commenced. The 1st Division, under Sir John Michel, were on their way to Tungchow.[5]

SOURCE NOTES

1 Royal Archives, Windsor Castle, RA VIC ADD MSS E/1, 2894.
2 Carter, T. L., *Historical Records of the 44th or East Essex Regiment*, W. O. Mitchell, 1864.
3 Atkinson, C. T., *Regimental History of the Royal Hampshire Regiment*, vol.1, University Press Glasgow, 1950.
4 Porter, Major-General W., *History of the Corps of Royal Engineers*, 1889.
5 Swinhoe, R., *Narrative of the North China Campaign*, Smith Elder, 1861.
6 Cantlie, Lieut-General Sir N., *A History of the Army Medical Department*, vol.2 1974.
7 Wolseley, Lieut-Colonel G. J., *Narrative of the War with China, 1860*, Longman, Green, Longman & Roberts, 1862.

8 Bruce Tulloch, Sir Alexander, *Recollections of Forty Years' Service*, Blackwood, 1903.

9 Bowlby, C. C., *An Account of the Last Mission and Death of Thomas William Bowlby*, private circulation, 1906.

10 Royal Archives, Windsor Castle, RA, VIC, ADD, MSS, E/1, 2835.

10

Lord Elgin and Baron Gros, the two ambassadors, accompanied the advancing troops, and on 11 September a despatch arrived from Peking saying that the previous Imperial Commissioners were being replaced and the new emissaries would leave Peking for Tientsin on the 12th; there was therefore no need for Lord Elgin to leave Tientsin, nor for the Allies to continue their advance. Elgin sent a reply to the effect that no treaty could be agreed before the Allies had reached Tungchow. On 12 September two further letters arrived, asking that the troops should return to Tientsin, where negotiations could be reopened. Both requests were refused.

The cavalry led the advance from Tientsin, the King's Dragoon Guards and Fane's Horse moving out on 8 September, followed by the rest of the advance guard, which was made up of the right wing of the 99th Regiment (Wiltshires) and 400 men of the Royal Marine Light Infantry, with Stirling's and Barry's batteries of the Royal Artillery in support. Brigadier Reeves was in command. Bowlby noted that 'The King's Dragoon Guards with their white helmets and scarlet coats were followed by Fane's Horse in their blue tunics and red turbans, the pennons on their lances streaming gaily in the wind.' On that first day's march Bowlby remembered that 'About 1 [o'clock] a tremendous thunderstorm burst right over us. The rain descended in buckets and lasted until 10 p.m.'[1]

The march was not easy for the cavalry because at that time of year in North China the main crop was millet, whose individual stalks, when cut, stood an inch in diameter and some six inches from the ground. The roads were equally difficult; the main thoroughfares were originally constructed of huge stone blocks, but they had not been maintained for many years with the result that stones had been removed, leaving large gaps and holes. The secondary roads were only mud, with cuttings deep enough to conceal both man and beast. These cuttings were often too wide for the cavalry to jump and too narrow to be able to scramble across. Grant commented, 'The country was excessively difficult for troops to advance along, and very dangerous for horses, as the fields were full of millet, which when cut, formed very sharp stalks in the ground, and injured them severely.'[2]

The cavalry had, however, come into their own, and Grant told the Duke of Cambridge:

I cannot say how thankful I am that Cavalry was sent from India with this force. I scarcely know how we should have got on without it, from the clouds of horsemen which encircled our small forces. And right gallantly the Tartar horse came at us and charged up nearly to our guns.[2]

The cavalry became victims of their own success, as more and more demands were made upon them for escorts and detachments, thus dissipating their strength. The King's Dragoon Guards had to provide escorts for the various diplomatic missions, together with orderly dragoons for the staff; Probyn's Horse provided an escort of twenty-five sabres for the Armstrong guns, another twenty-five for the lines of communication at Yangtsun, and 100 men for the diplomatic missions; whilst Fane's Horse had to detach a complete squadron to the French, who had no cavalry of their own except for General de Montauban's small escort. Swinhoe wrote:

It could not have been deemed arrogant for a British officer to admire the drill and turn-out of the Sikhs, as compared to the wretched Spahis from Algeria of the French lines, who too often showed themselves impatient of discipline, as the French officers acknowledged, and were mounted on the most wretched of Manila ponies, lank and half-starved to look at.[3]

Hosiwu was reached on 13 September and was found to be practically deserted, for the local Chinese, who up to this point had been friendly and helpful, now fled on the approach of the advancing troops.

There were two very large pawnbrokers' shops there, containing great quantities of warm clothing and valuables of all sorts. We placed guards over them, but the Chinese thieves climbed over the walls and roof tops at night, and succeeded in carrying off property without being perceived. When this was discovered, all the Chinese remaining in the town were ordered to quit forthwith, in order to save what remained. We procured delicious grapes and very good vegetables there, and the large quantities of yams and sweet potatoes growing in the surrounding fields enabled our army to feed well. Hosiwu is closely surrounded by orchards of peach, apple and pear trees.[4]

Captain Hart Dunne of the 99th Regiment (Wiltshires),with other officers, hunted wild pig in the locality, following their Medical Officer's hounds.[5]

In spite of the precautions taken to guard Chinese property, a certain amount of looting took place, with some of the officers acquiring mandarins' coats, and the men found too much rice wine and bad brandy. The best efforts of the Provost Marshal, with the frequent use of his cane, and the extreme displeasure expressed by Grant in a general order never completely stopped this pilfering.

Grant had decided to establish a depot. The Pei-ho river was navigable as far as Hosiwu, but during the summer months the level of water did not allow junks to go much beyond the town. In addition, the change in attitude of the local Chinese made the availability of local provisions very much more uncertain. A field hospital was also set up, and the sick or wounded were then evacuated down the river to Tientsin as soon as possible. Admiral Hope had formed a number of flotillas of junks, consisting of between sixty to eighty junks in each flotilla, with a commander from the Royal Navy in charge of each flotilla and a number of other naval officers to assist him. Hope also placed a British sailor on board each junk. The siege train of heavy artillery was floated up the river to Hosiwu on pontoons. For the first few days a small escort of troops marched along the banks of the Pei-ho with each flotilla as it made its way up river, but after a few days this precaution was found to be unnecessary.

Grant took a few days to bring forward the British and French troops from Tientsin; the French arrived at Hosiwu on 14 September and pitched their camp beyond that of the British; Probyn's Horse left Tientsin with the 1st Division on the 12th and reached Hosiwu on 16 September. The 1st Division now had with them the 2nd Regiment (Queen's), the 15th Punjabis, and Desborough's battery of the Royal Artillery.

On 13 September Bowlby 'found Parkes who came on last night with Walker, twenty KDG's and fifty Sowars'.[1] That afternoon Parkes with Wade and an escort of twenty cavalry went forward to Matow, a village twelve miles from Hosiwu on the road to Peking, in order to meet the new Imperial Commissioners. On reaching Matow, they found that the Chinese had returned to Tungchow, apparently feeling that they had allowed themselves to come too close to the Allied army. Parkes and Wade then rode on to Tungchow, arriving on the 14th to meet the Imperial Commissioners. After lengthy bargaining it was agreed that the Allies should advance to fwithin a short distance of Chang-kia-wan, where they should halt; Lord Elgin, with an escort of 1,000 men, would then proceed to Tungchow, where he would meet the Imperial Commissioners, sign the Convention, and then move on to Peking with his escort in order to ratify the treaty of 1848, which had been the cause of the present dispute.

Bowlby had 'a long talk with Lord Elgin' on 16 September:

The Imperial Commissioners state broadly that he [Lord Elgin] had been humbugged, both in 1848 and at Tientsin this month. [The new Imperial Commissioners] are the first men in the Empire, and therefore implicit reliance may be placed on their words, – i.e. that past duplicity is a guarantee of future good faith. They agreed to [a] Convention if [the] army stopped. Lord Elgin replies that the army marches tomorrow towards Tungchow and, if opposed, would crush any force that might venture to attack it; that it will stop [short of] Chang-kia-wan, [by] between 4 or 5 miles; that the Commissioners must publish a proclamation stating that it was at their

request the march was stopped as negotiations had begun, informing the people that they would not be plundered and requesting
them to bring in supplies; that he would go to Tungchow, with
2,000 men, to sign [the] Convention and afterwards to Peking to
ratify [the] treaty of Tientsin and present letters to the Emperor;
that from their own admissions it was clear that they yielded to
force, and to force alone, and therefore it would depend on
circumstances how soon the troops would be withdrawn from
Tientsin.

Elgin then informed Grant of the results of his negotiations.[1]

The fact that Elgin accompanied the force with full political powers, and that it was he and his subordinates from the
Diplomatic and Consular Service who carried out all the
negotiations with the Chinese, led to a good deal of grumbling among the officers and troops. To the soldiers it seemed
clear that the 'politicals' were again being deceived, and since
military advice was not sought, the sending of 2,000 men, on
their own, into the enemy's capital city appeared to them to
be risking soldiers' lives on the flimsiest of evidence.

Grant decided to leave the 2nd Regiment (The Queen's) as
garrison at Hosiwu, to protect the stores and hospital,
together with twenty-five sowars of Probyn's Horse who
formed the escort to the three Armstrong guns, which would
also remain. As Elgin was staying at Hosiwu, his escort of
100 sowars of Probyn's remained with him.

On 17 September Parkes and Mr Loch, Private Secretary to
Elgin, set out very early from Hosiwu for Tungchow to make
the arrangements for Elgin to follow. They were accompa-
nied by Colonel Walker, Quartermaster General of the
Cavalry Brigade, Mr Thompson, a Commissariat officer, Mr
De Norman and Bowlby. Their escort was commanded by
Lieutenant Anderson of Fane's Horse, who had twenty-five
sowars of his regiment and five troopers of the King's Dragoon
Guards. At daybreak Grant broke camp and the Allied force set
out for Matow. That evening the force was joined at Matow by
the 2nd Regiment (The Queen's), who had been relieved at
Hosiwu by the 60th Rifles and had at once started out to rejoin
the force.

On 18 September the troops left Matow for Chang-Kia-Wan. Having marched for about three miles, the advance guard suddenly came upon a picket of Chinese cavalry, who immediately fled. A few miles further on the advance guard came up against a large Chinese army, stretching across a front of some five miles and barring the way forward. Grant at once halted the Allied force, ordered the baggage to concentrate in the last village through which they had passed, and sent an officer of the King's Dragoon Guards to close up the rearguard for their protection. By this time the Tartar cavalry was working around the flanks of the Allied force, and considerable Chinese infantry reinforcements could be seen moving into position alongside large batteries of guns.

The troops had not been halted for long when Loch, escorted by three sowars of Fane's Horse, galloped into the Allied lines from Parkes's party. They brought the news that Parkes, Colonel Walker and Commissary Thompson, together with five troopers of the King's Dragoon Guards and four sowars of Fane's Horse, had left Tungchow shortly after 5 a.m. to mark out the area of the Allied camp in front of Chang-kia-wan. Loch brought letters from Parkes saying that a satisfactory agreement had been reached with the Imperial Commissioners, but he also brought the news that, on their way back, they had passed 'large bodies' of Chinese troops, together with many batteries of artillery, in the vicinity of Chang-kia-wan, and in areas where no troops had been seen previously. He said that Lieutenant Anderson, Bowlby and De Norman, with the rest of the escort, seventeen sowars from Fane's Horse, had stayed behind at Tungchow.

When Parkes, Colonel Walker and their party arrived at Chang-kia-wan and saw the strength of the Chinese army in the area, Colonel Walker was left in charge of the party, with orders to stay in the vicinity of Chang-kia-wan and to observe the Chinese movements and dispositions. Parkes himself, taking Private Phipps of the King's Dragoon Guards as his single orderly, returned at once to Tungchow to demand an explanation from the Imperial Commissioners. These actions left Grant in a difficult position; Parkes was on his way back to

Tungchow, where Anderson and his sowars had remained, and Walker was in the midst of an apparently hostile Chinese army. In effect, the Chinese had some thirty hostages in their power. In the meantime the Tartar horse was enveloping Grant's force, and he was faced by a Chinese army that heavily outnumbered his own in both troops and guns.

Loch at once volunteered to return to Tungchow, carrying an order from Grant directing all of Parkes's original party back into the lines. Captain Brabazon of the Royal Artillery offered to accompany Loch, and at eight o'clock the two men set out with an escort of two sowars from Probyn's Horse, Nihal Singh and Bargir Jowahir, carrying a white flag of truce.

Grant had with him at Chang-kia-wan the Cavalry Brigade, commanded by Brigadier Pattle, less their various detachments on other duties, and consisting of the King's Dragoon Guards, Probyn's Horse and Fane's Horse supported by Stirling's half-battery; elements of two infantry brigades under Brigadiers Reeves and Sutton, made up of the 2nd Regiment (The Queen's), 99th Regiment (Wiltshires), Royal Marine Light Infantry and the 15th Punjabis; and two batteries of the Royal Artillery under Captain Desborough, together with detachments of the Royal Engineers and the Military Train. The French had the 2nd Chasseurs de Vincennes and one battery of field artillery up with the force, which, since it was intended as the escort to Lord Elgin under the original arrangements, totalled less than 2,000 men.

Grant sent his cavalry out on to both flanks, to keep himself informed of the Chinese moves, but gave them strict orders not to become involved in any action. Grant himself took up a position close by the road on top of a small mound, and some 400 yards from the Chinese position; he could clearly see the red coats of the five troopers of the King's Dragoon Guards in Colonel Walker's party moving about in the midst of the grey-clad Chinese. Shortly afterwards one of the Imperial Commissioners appeared under a flag of truce, asking to speak to Lord Elgin, but when he was told that Lord Elgin was back at Hosiwu, he returned to his own lines. Before he left, Grant asked him the reason for the Tartar cavalry gathering on the flanks, and was told that they were merely gathering supplies for the Allied force. Next a Chinese officer with three men arrived, saying that he had come to show the Allies where they were to camp. Grant continued to stay where he was, awaiting the return of Parkes and his party.

After two to three hours of waiting, at between ten and eleven o'clock, there was a stir in the Chinese lines and suddenly Colonel Walker and a group of horsemen were seen galloping through the Chinese surrounding them, and heading for the Allied position. At the same time the Chinese opened fire with gingals and artillery along the length of their line. On arrival the party was found to consist of Colonel Walker, Assistant Commissary Thompson and two troopers of the King's Dragoon Guards. Colonel Walker related how he had been shown a position for camp right in the midst of the Chinese troops, and when he had tried to indicate that any camp site must be nearer to water, he was left waiting. As they waited, the attitude of the Chinese surrounding them began to change from civility to rudeness, particularly as more and more Chinese reinforcements came up. At this point Colonel Walker warned his companions that they might have to make a dash for it back to their own lines, and in the meantime they were to be very careful not to give offence and to avoid any show of hostility. A Chinese mandarin, who may have been Sankolinsin, rode by surrounded by a strong escort, but the mandarin turned his head away and pretended not to see the British officers. Then a group of Chinese soldiers crowded round Walker and one of them suddenly tilted Walker's scabbard so that the sword came out and was immediately seized. A Chinese officer nearby reprimanded the man and had Walker's sword returned to him.

Shortly after this Walker saw a French officer, who had accompanied the party to Tungchow, surrounded by a mob of Chinese soldiers. Seeing Walker, the Frenchman called out to him for assistance, and when Walker reached him he saw that he had a deep sabre cut on his head and more wounds on his body. Walker grasped his hand and tried to lead him away, but as he did so the Chinese rushed at them, knocked the French officer down, dragged Walker's sword out of its scabbard and at the same time tried to pull him off his horse. Walker, in trying to rescue his sword, cut his hand badly and then shouted to his companions to ride for their lives. As the party put spurs to their horses, the Chinese opened fire on them from every side, but only succeeded in wounding two of the men and in shooting one horse.

The Chinese kept up their fire and General de Montauban suggested to Grant that the French, who were on the right of the Allied line, and numbered 1,000 men of the 2nd Chasseurs de Vincennes and the few Spahis of the General's escort, should attack the Chinese position to their immediate front. De Montauban placed Colonel Foley, the British Commissioner with the French, in charge of the attack, and Grant sent a squadron of Fane's Horse, under command of Lieutenant Cattley, to supplement the few French Spahis. The Chasseurs carried the enemy's works in dashing style, while the cavalry swept around the position, charging three times against the Chinese and doing great execution.

Between the French on the right and the British centre there was some rising ground, where Grant placed Desborough's nine-pounders supported by a squadron of the King's Dragoon Guards. The centre of the Allied line was held by the 15th Punjabis and the 99th Regiment (Wiltshires), who pushed forward two companies under Major Dowbiggin to occupy some houses immediately in front of the Chinese position. The 99th were ordered to advance straight up the road towards the Chinese, and they were given the support of two nine-pounder guns. The 15th Punjabis on the left of the 99th had the support of the Armstrong guns, while on the left flank the 2nd Queen's were to follow up Probyn's Horse and the rest of the King's Dragoon Guards with the Armstrong guns of Stirling's battery.

The Allied artillery fire soon began to silence the Chinese batteries and scatter the infantry. The Tartar horse had gathered in great numbers on the Allied left flank, and as Probyn's Horse led the movement on that flank, they found themselves faced with more than 2,000 Tartar horse. That day

Probyn's mustered only 106 sabres and by now the regiment was far out in front. Without hesitation Probyn gave the order to charge and the small line of Sikh horsemen cut straight into the mass of Chinese cavalry, breaking through them and then, wheeling, charging back through them a second time. Grant reported:

Sir John Michel encountered such heavy masses on his left that he had some difficulty in holding his position, and was attacked by a large body of Tartar cavalry. Probyn, who had only 100 of his Regiment with him at the time, was ordered to charge to the front, which he did in most gallant style, riding in amongst them with such vigour and determination that they could not withstand his attack for a moment, and fled in utter consternation.[9]

Sir John Michel added his praise: 'The charge was gallantly executed and eminently successful, and I cannot speak too highly of the bravery of this small party and the merit of its commander.' Probyn's and the King's Dragoon Guards, who had now come up in their support, chased the fleeing Tartars for several miles. An old Sikh sowar was heard to remark afterwards that the Tartars were like so many chicken, very difficult to overtake and absolutely harmless when caught.[6]

The 15th Punjabis carried the Chinese lines to their front in great style. Grant described their advance:

The Musbees [a low caste of Sikh, who made up the 15th Punjabis] then advanced in a steady line carrying everything before them, and taking several guns. By-and-by we were joined by the 99th Regiment, the nine-pounder battery and the [rest of the] Dragoon Guards; and Sir John Michel having sent to say that the enemy was still very strong in front of him, I sent the Armstrong battery to his assistance, and shortly after they retired.[9]

As the Chinese retreated from Chang-kia-wan, and the infantry advanced, the numerous Chinese camps dotted about the area were destroyed. The walled town of Chang-kia-wan was occupied by the British, while the French camped outside. More than eighty guns had been captured and it was estimated that Sankolinsin's force had numbered some 20,000 men. The Allied casualties had been light, the French losing some fifteen men and the British twenty; the King's Dragoon Guards had two troopers wounded, Phillips and Collingwood, with one horse shot and one troop horse wounded. The French had the colonel commanding their Spahi cavalry killed in the charge with Fane's Horse. General de Montauban was so delighted with the performance of Fane's Squadron that Lieutenant Cattley, its commander, was awarded the Legion of Honour, and Lieutenants Fitzgerald, Upperton and Lake were commended. Fane's lost one NCO killed, with two NCOs and two sowars wounded.[7,8]

In spite of the victory there was a feeling of despondency in the Allied camp that night. The fate of the missing men, both of Parkes's party, and of Loch and Brabazon, was not known, but it was feared that the Chinese might take revenge for their defeat upon the wretched men. The town of Chang-kia-wan was given over to plunder. The 99th Regiment (Wiltshires) put out pickets in front of the town, occupying the farthest Chinese camps which were left intact. Captain Hart Dunne, with more than half of the 99th, occupied the centre picket, where they found that the Chinese straw huts were full of gunpowder. However, the men were able to eat plenty of sweet potatoes and half-cooked chicken found lying about. Next day these rations were supplemented by their foraging more poultry and some sheep.[5]

SOURCE NOTES

1 Bowlby, C. C., *An Account of the Last Mission and Death of Thomas William Bowlby*, private circulation, 1906.
2 Royal Archives, Windsor Castle, RA VIC ADD MSS E/1, 2835.
3 Swinhoe, R., *Narrative of the North China Campaign*, Smith Elder, 1861.
4 Wolseley, Lieut-Colonel G. J., *Narrative of the War with China, 1860*, Longman, Green, Longman & Roberts, 1862.
5 Kenrick, Colonel N. C. E., *The Story of the Wiltshire Regiment*, Gale & Polden, 1963.
6 Boyle, Major A. C., *History of Probyn's Horse*, Gale & Polden, 1929.

7 Records of the King's Dragoon Guards, Regimental Museum of 1st The Queen's Dragoon Guards, Cardiff Castle.

8 Hudson, General Sir H., *History of the 19th King George's Own Lancers, 1858–1921*, Gale & Polden, 1937.

9 Knollys H., *Incidents in the China War of 1869*, Blackwood, 1875.

II

Wolseley described the sack of Chang-kia-wan:

It was a strange sight, for the two following days, to see the crowds of poor people from the surrounding villages pouring in from daybreak until dark for the purpose of sharing in the plunder. To them, the clothes and furniture, which, in the pawn-shops particularly, were stored in quantities, were of great value, although to our men they were of no use. I did not hear of any valuables being found; but in one warehouse there were about five million pounds of brick tea. This, as also our captured guns, we were unable to remove from want of carriage.[1]

Swinhoe also watched the looting:

Some hairy old Sikh, attired in feminine costume, would stroke his beard and strut in long boots before the admiring eyes of his surrounding comrades. In a walled enclosure several of the cavalry horses that had escaped their riders during the engagement were found; and curious enough, in a house hard by lay Colonel Walker's much valued sword, which had been snatched from that gallant officer.[2]

One of the chaplains, the Revd McGhee, became concerned for the fate of some of the Chinese women left behind by their menfolk. In one house a group of women and children were found who had attempted to commit suicide by taking overdoses of opium. They were taken in hand by one of the doctors, who managed to save the lives of all bar one, by keeping them moving and by dousing them with water. Another woman, on being brought into a central place for safety, tried to strangle her daughter rather than let her fall into the hands of the barbarians. All these well-intentioned efforts to protect the women came to naught when, as darkness fell, they made their escape into the surrounding countryside.

On 19 September Grant sent Mr Wade to Tungchow under a flag of truce, demanding that all British and French prisoners should be returned; if this did not happen at once, the Allies would attack Peking. Wade was not able to find out any reliable news of the captives at Tungchow, and so went on towards Peking. He had not gone far when he came across the Chinese army, whose outposts would not allow him to come any nearer; when he tried to approach them, they opened fire on him. Lord Elgin, who was still at Hosiwu, had heard the noise of the engagement at Chang-kia-wan, but did not receive Grant's report of the action until midnight of that day. On the morning of 19 September Elgin set out for Chang-kia-wan, and arrived there in the afternoon, immediately going with Grant to General de Montauban's quarters to decide on how best to secure the release of the prisoners. It was agreed that the cavalry should carry out a reconnaissance the next day.

On the 20th the cavalry probed forward and found a very strong Chinese force occupying a position in front of the Yang-Liang canal, which connected the Pei-ho river with Peking. The canal was crossed by two bridges, the first a wooden one, the other built of marble about one mile to the east and called Palichao, or Eight Li Bridge. During this reconnaissance a prisoner was captured who gave the news that the Chinese army was commanded by Sankolinsin in person. He also said that a number of foreign prisoners had been taken in carts to Peking on 18 September.

The French had taken advantage of the pause at Chang-kia-wan to move up more of their infantry from Hosiwu, and on the 20th General Collineau's brigade and a field battery of artillery reached the forward troops, bringing up the French strength to about 3,000 men. Both the British and French baggage parties were grouped together and placed under a strong guard, in preparation for an advance the next day.

The plan was that the French should take the right and seize the Palichao bridge, whilst the 1st Division under Sir John Michel should attack the wooden bridge, which was about a mile nearer to Peking. In the meantime the cavalry were to make a wide sweep to the left flank in order to drive the Chinese right flank in onto its centre, and force the enemy to retreat over the Yang-Liang canal by either the Palichao or the wooden bridge. It was hoped that this would crowd the Chinese army onto the two bridges, where it could be destroyed or severely mauled.

The Cavalry Brigade and the 1st Division set out from Chang-kia-wan at daybreak on 21 September, but they had advanced for only two miles when a halt had to be called to allow the French infantry time to move into position on the right flank. Swinhoe was ordered to take the place of the missing Parkes as interpreter to Grant. He found the General dismounted and conferring with his officers in the shade of a wood, while his escort of Sikhs from Probyn's Horse also stood leisurely around. They were soon joined by Lord Elgin and his staff, and an escort of dragoons from the King's Dragoon Guards. After some time the French arrived, having been delayed by the baggage obstructing the streets of Chang-kia-wan, and the two forces started to advance. They had only marched for a mile when they were confronted by the whole Chinese army. The Tartar cavalry was in great strength on the right of the Chinese position; the Chinese Imperial infantry and artillery were posted in and around the numerous clumps of trees and enclosures of millet which lay between the Allies and the Yang-Liang canal. On this occasion the Imperial army was drawn up under the strict central control of General Sankolinsin, with the Chinese infantry acting as a central pivot, plentifully supported by artillery, and with the cavalry moving in well-drilled squadrons to provide the mobile striking force.[2]

As soon as the Allies came within range, the Chinese artillery and gingals opened fire, whereupon the French unlimbered their guns and started to reply. The Tartar cavalry began to move forward in two masses, one advancing towards the gap between the French on their left and the British centre, while the other massed on the right immediately started an outflanking movement of the British left. Grant, who was with his staff, wrote:

Our troops were formed up with the infantry on the right, artillery in the centre, and cavalry in echelon on the left, and I then rode up to the French to reconnoitre the position of the enemy. As I was quietly riding back, I saw some cavalry on the left front of our allies, which I at first took for some of their skirmishers, when they suddenly approached me, and I found they were Tartars.[3]

Swinhoe, who was with Grant, wrote:

Sir Hope Grant, followed by his staff, rode towards the French lines to confer with General Montauban as to the order of attack. A few words were exchanged, and the British General moved slowly forward in advance of the column, apparently engaged in thought, and without taking heed of a line of Tartar cavalry drawn up ahead on the farther side of a long mound. The Mandarin in command was observed riding up and down in front of his men, and inspiriting them to the charge; and when we approached to within two hundred yards, the Tartars gave a series of yells, and leaping the bank, charged furiously at us, discharging their matchlocks.[2]

Grant himself continues: 'I immediately galloped off to Stirling's guns, and opened fire with case at a range of 200 yards, which quickly made them retire.'[3] Swinhoe gives some more detail:

The General and Staff at once galloped off to the right and left, disclosing the Armstrongs, which wheeled around in hot haste and unlimbered, giving, however, to the Tartars the impression that all hands were panic stricken and turning tail. They, therefore, galloped forward the more boldly, cheering and uttering their war cries, but before they had proceeded far the case shot poured in among them, and the rifles of the 2nd Queen's saluted them with a shower of bullets. Their cheers soon yielded to yells of despair as they hastily withdrew to a more respectful distance.[2]

Wolseley had some comments to make about the accuracy of the Queen's rifle fire:

An infantry battalion close by was ordered by its Brigadier to form square, and in that formation fired volleys at the advancing enemy, without, I believe, killing a man of them. Our old soldiers, untrained in all the minutiae of position and judging-distance drill, and armed with the much-abused Brown Bess, could not certainly have done less damage.[1]

Sidney Herbert commented to Queen Victoria:

The French musketry fire was very superior to ours at close quarters, which he [Grant] attributes to their rifles having no sights. The men in action got hurried and confused and could not lower the long range sights, and thus fire over the heads of the enemy. The French rifles with sights are reserved for picked men only, as skirmishers.[5]

Grant continued:

The King's Dragoon Guards and Fane's Horse, with Probyn's regiment in support, now advanced to the charge; the first-named taking a bank and ditch on their way, and, attacking the Tartars with the utmost vigour, instantly made them give way. Fane's men followed them in pursuit, and on reaching the margin of a road jumped into it over an interposing high bank and ditch. The front rank cleared it well; but the men in rear, unable to see before them owing to the excessive dust, almost all rolled into the ditch. Nevertheless, the Tartars had but a poor chance, and suffered severely. The whole of their cavalry retreated, and we followed them up for some time, occasionally firing long shots at them with our Armstrongs with good effect.[3]

Wolseley witnessed the cavalry charge:

Our cavalry, which had been moving slowly forwards in that direction, went straight at them, Fane's Horse and the King's Dragoon Guards in the first line, Probyn's regiment in support behind. The Tartar cavalry had halted behind a deep wide ditch, upon seeing our troops advancing towards them, from which position they delivered a volley as our cavalry reached it. The horses of the irregulars are always ridden in short standing martingales, which effectively prevent their jumping well; so, when our line reached the ditch, but very few of the irregulars got over it at first, many of their horses, unable to pull up, tumbling in, one over the other. The King's Dragoon Guards, however, got well in among the Tartars, riding over ponies and men, and knocking both down together like so many ninepins. The irregulars were soon after them, and in the short pursuit which then ensued, the wild Pathans of Fane's Horse showed well fighting side by side with the powerful British Dragoon. The result was most satisfactory. Riderless Tartar horses were to be seen galloping about in all directions, and the ground passed over in the charge was well strewn with the enemy. At no time subsequently during the day would they allow our cavalry sufficiently near for a second charge. Our artillery opened fire upon the retreating forces with good effect, firing slowly, every Armstrong shell bursting among them and bringing down the enemy in clumps.[1]

In a later account Wolseley remembered that the Chinese

were mounted on small ponies, our men on great troop horses. The men of the King's Dragoon Guards were then about the biggest of our cavalry of the Line, and as they went thundering forward with loud shouts, their opponents may well have thought that their last hour had come. Probyn's and Fane's sharp-sworded Sikhs, Pathans and Punjabi-Mussulmen showed splendidly, fighting side by side with the big sturdy British Dragoon Guardsmen.[6]

Trumpeter John Goldsworthy of the King's Dragoon Guards was orderly trumpeter to Sir John Michel, commanding the 1st Division, and took part in the charge:

On the morning of the 21st September, 1860, being trumpeter to General Sir John Michel, I was ordered to rejoin my Regiment which was about to charge the enemy. This we carried out in excellent style, notwithstanding the difficult nature of the ground, and I had disposed of some six or seven of the enemy, when I noticed that Lieutenant W. S. McLeod, of the Madras Cavalry, who was attached to my Regiment for duty, was surrounded by seven or eight Tartars, one of whom was preparing to give him a final stroke, when I pierced him through the neck, killing him instantly. I then turned my attention to the others, and succeeded in killing, or mortally wounding, them all, thus saving the Officer's life. I followed in the pursuit and managed to slay three Mandarins, and, catching the eye of (then) Lieutenant Marsland (now General and late Colonel of the 5th Dragoon Guards), remarked to him: 'That's the way to polish them off, Sir!' He replied: 'Well done, Trumpeter, go on and polish some more off.' I did so, but on coming to a halt, as soon as the smoke had cleared away, found that I was simply in the midst of the Chinese Army. I resolved to clear myself, so putting spurs to my horse, I made a dash and rode straight through them about a mile and a half in the direction of my Regiment, which I found formed up for the roll-call. I had to cut my way right and left to get back through the Tartar army as I did, and my trumpet was shot off my back, but I calculated that forty six fell to my sword that day. I recovered my trumpet the next day, it having been found by one of Probyn's Horse, and on unrolling my cloak from my saddle four bullets fell out.

The reason for this was probably because the Chinese soldiers, having difficulty in ramming the bullets down the barrels of their matchlocks, filed down the slugs to make them fit more easily, with the result that, when fired, the bullet had no force behind it.[7] Swinhoe related how both the Chinese and the British

were withdrawn from view by the cloud of dust that enveloped them, and nought could be seen of the encounter save an occasional gleam of the uplifted sword, or puffs of grey smoke from the discharged carbine or pistol. In a minute, as it were, the cloud of dust was swept away, and the gallant Dragoons appeared drawn up in line, as if nothing had happened.

We soon moved over the ground. One Private lay dead of a matchlock-ball wound through the heart, and a Captain of Dragoons dropped to the rear with a bad cut on his arm: but the ground was strewn with dead and dying Tartars. I stopped with the Commander-in-Chief's Doctor to look at the dead Private. As his face was turned upwards, one Dragoon that stood near remarked to another, 'Why, Bill, if it ain't old Charley! Poor fellow! He has gone to his long home!'[2]

The wounded KDG captain was Captain Bradbury, and the dead trooper was Private Webster. The King's Dragoon Guards also had Privates Napier and Davis severely wounded, and Privates Lawrence, Hughes, Ductat, Mason and Pollett slightly wounded in the charge, with a total of eight horses missing. Pollett later died of his wound.[8]

Grant reported on the rest of the action:

We continued our advance until we were stopped by a force firing at us from a strong position in a village and from a tope of trees. We soon, however, brought up some infantry [2nd Regiment, The Queen's] and dislodged them without difficulty. It must have formed the camping ground of a Tartar General of some importance, as we there captured two yellow silk banners belonging to the Imperial Guard, one of which I have now in my possession; eighteen brass guns likewise here fell into our possession. The French attacked the bridge of Palichao with great gallantry. The elite of the Chinese Imperial Guard was drawn up to resist them, but had to give way before European discipline. The French took with the bridge twenty-five guns.[3]

Sankolinsin exercised a central control over his army, transmitting his orders by the waving of banners. The main one, coloured yellow and black, was wielded by a huge Tartar standing on top of the Palichao bridge, whom the French dispatched with great efficiency.

Wolseley remembered how

Sir Hope Grant with the Cavalry, three Armstrong guns, the 99th Regiment [Wiltshires], and Royal Marines moved in pursuit to our left, in which direction we found several camps. The ground was difficult in some places for cavalry and artillery. In one of the captured camps we found eighteen guns, and in all the tents were standing. Of course we burnt and destroyed all we took. As we approached each camp, we could see the enemy streaming out from it, and only in one instance did they attempt any resistance. Our cavalry having approached an encampment which was closely surrounded with trees and broken ground, where they were of course powerless against the enemy's infantry, which opening a sharp fire, several of our men were wounded. When, however, our infantry and artillery came up, the enemy were quickly dislodged, and the 99th suceeded in bayoneting several. Our pursuit lasted to within about six miles of Peking, horses and men being well tired and hungry. The enemy having disappeared from our front and flank, we marched back, making for the wooden bridge over the canal where we rejoined the 2nd Brigade.[1]

Probyn's Horse did in fact carry out a second charge, which apparently did not meet with the approval of Brigadier Pattle, commanding the Cavalry Brigade. Swinhoe relates how during the advance

Probyn's Horse took a circuit well to the left, and tried to get round the enemy. We at first lost sight of them. Presently a line of serried pennons appeared in the distance, with a peculiar quivering motion. They moved nearer and nearer, and soon we could make out that it was the gallant Major and his trusty sabres. They made for a large party of Tartars bustling about under some trees, and charged at them. The Tartars scuttled away in confusion.[2]

Probyn's Regimental History comments:

Probyn saw an opportunity which he thought demanded action, and he at once took the chance of delivering an effective charge. Sir Hope

Grant personally witnessed this charge, and in direct contradiction of the Brigadier's opinion, described it as 'admirable'.[9]

Swinhoe includes a gruesome detail:

In one of the charges of the Sikh cavalry, a trooper lost the management of his horse, and was carried among the enemy, who first gouged his eyes out in a most barbarous manner, and then cut him to pieces, limb by limb.[2]

At this point Grant felt that

The enemy had apparently disappeared, and I retired towards the bridge, where our camp was being pitched, when suddenly fire was opened on us from the other side, whereupon the Musbees crossed the canal, took the guns, and killed sixty of the enemy.[3]

Wolseley relates how

Colonel Mackenzie, our Quartermaster General, was marking out the position for our camp, [when] a fire was suddenly opened by the enemy from the north bank of the canal. A party of the 15th Punjabi Infantry under Lieutenant Harris, the second in command of that Corps, was immediately pushed across the river, supported by a wing of the 2nd Queen's. The Punjabis advanced most dashingly, driving the enemy from a camp which stood near the canal and capturing the guns from which they had opened fire.[1]

Swinhoe saw

The 15th Punjabis and two howitzers [who] were ordered to cross the river and put a stop to the annoyance. They came upon a camp of troops robed in Imperial yellow, with silk banners of the same colour. These soon decamped, and their camp was destroyed; but our troops soon afterwards came to close quarters with some Tartars in a village, and committed great havoc among them. One gallant Punjabi Officer, forgetting the use of the sword that hung by his side, engaged a Tartar with closed fists, and had succeeded in flooring him, when a Punjabi private thrust the man through with his bayonet.[2]

After the battle the Sikh troopers of Probyn's and Fane's Horse rode over the battlefield,

and it was common practice among these gentlemen to murder the wounded. As they rode past a prostrate wounded man, one would prick him with a spear's point, and, if the unfortunate sufferer cried out or writhed under the pain inflicted, some of the party would dismount and deliberately saw his head off.[2]

Grant continued, 'We finally encamped upon some high ground on the right bank of the canal, and the French on the other side, near the Palichao bridge.'[3] Swinhoe

was then sent with an Officer and a guard of Sikh troopers to bring up the baggage, which was halted at a village some way in the rear of the camping ground. We found the baggagers in great alarm, as they had mistaken us at a distance for a squadron of the enemy's cavalry.

They were soon, however, reassured and eventually reached in safety the grove of trees that marked the picturesque spot on the banks of the canal where the camp was to be fixed.[2]

Wolseley remembered:

Our baggage, which had been sent for when the pursuit ended, came up in the afternoon. I should imagine that almost every man in our army ate ducks for dinner that evening; for upon arriving at the canal it was crowded with fine large ducks, which so quickly disappeared, that the next morning, when going there to bathe, I could only see four remaining. Our loss in men during the day had been only two killed and twenty-nine wounded; our allies also only suffered slightly.[1]

The burden of the casualties had been borne by the cavalry, the KDG had one man killed, one officer and seven men wounded, Probyn's had one man killed, and Fane's one officer and thirteen men wounded. The total infantry casualties were eight men wounded.

Grant, in reporting the action to the Duke of Cambridge, commented:

I am happy to say in the last fight the 1st Dragoon Guards did very well and charged into a troop of Tartars riding over a ditch and bank on the way and killing a great many.

I beg also to speak in the most favourable terms of the Armstrong guns. The precision of their fire at great distance is most admirable, and if the fuzes were as good, the execution they would do would be great.[4]

Sidney Herbert, in reporting to the Queen, was most enthusiastic:

The charge of the King's Dragoon Guards was an act of horsemanship most remarkable. The Tartars were posted on an elevated mound with a deep ditch in front, and the Horse had not only to clear the ditch, but to leap up the height at the same time. Only one man was unhorsed. The Sikh cavalry tried to do it, but upwards of thirty saddles were immediately empty. On looking at this and another obstacle with a deep drop which the Dragoon Guards passed, he [Grant] says it is impossible to conceive how cavalry could do it.[5]

Trumpeter Goldsworthy of the King's Dragoon Guards was recommended for the Victoria Cross for his gallant action in saving the life of Lieutenant McLeod, but the recommendation was turned down. Two years later, when the regiment was back in India, Lieutenant McLeod's brother joined the KDG, and brought with him a gold watch and chain from McLeod, which he presented to Goldsworthy in gratitude for saving his brother's life. Lieutenant (later General) Marsland, who had witnessed the affair, tried for many years to gain recognition for this gallant deed, and eventually, thirty-six years later, Goldsworthy, then a saddler sergeant in the 3rd Hussars, was awarded an additional pension of sixpence a day.[7]

SOURCES

1 Wolseley, Lieut-Colonel G. J., *Narrative of the War with China, 1860*, Longman, Green, Longman & Roberts, 1862.
2 Swinhoe, R., *Narrative of the North China Campaign*, Smith Elder, 1861.
3 Knollys, H., *Incidents in the China War of 1860*, Blackwood, 1875.
4 Royal Archives, Windsor Castle, RA VIC ADD MSS E/1, 2835.
5 Royal Archives, Windsor Castle, RA VIC ADD MSS E/1, Q 15.
6 Wolseley, Lieut-Colonel G. J., *The Story of a Soldier's Life*, London, 1903.
7 *The Cavalry Journal*, vol.18, 1928, p.647.
8 Records of the King's Dragoon Guards, Regimental Museum of 1st The Queen's Dragoon Guards, Cardiff Castle.
9 Boyle, Major A. C., *History of Probyn's Horse*, Gale & Polden, 1929.

12

Grant wrote to the Duke of Cambridge from the camp after the battle:

We must wait here for reinforcements for a few days. General Montauban has written to his King for more troops and a heavy battery; and our siege guns and mortars will be up very shortly. We get our commissariat supplies up by junks, but as yet we have been most usefully supplied from the country, though I regret to say we have been obliged to take anything, the people of the neighbourhood having almost all fled from their houses. A note has been made of anything, and they will be repaid as soon as the war is over. At present we are encamped almost 3 miles beyond Tungchow, and we have promised not to allow the soldiers to go into the town, which at present has not been deserted, provided supplies are brought out and a market established in the neighbourhood of the camp, which has been promised by the Mandarin Magistrate, and which I trust will be carried out.[1]

Grant had with him only the 1st Division and the Cavalry Brigade from the British troops, together with some 3,000 French infantry, and he did not feel that this was an adequate force with which to assault Peking, especially as he had only advanced with such slight strength, against his will, at the behest of the diplomats. He was determined not to be caught out a second time, and sent for the 2nd Division and for the siege train to join him. Wolseley commented:

Although we had in the space of three days gained two battles, our position at Palichao was far from satisfactory. Our force was very small, and unprovided with the material required for a siege. Our heavy guns were still on the river, and great difficulty was experienced in getting them over the shallows. Before leaving Hosiwu, it was unfortunately believed that all the fighting was over, and that the Chinese Government was anxious for peace. Had it been otherwise, and the whole affair a purely military operation, we should never have left that place until our heavy guns and all available troops had reached it. As it was, relying upon the negotiations then pending, we advanced with a small force, unprepared for a siege; so that when our diplomacy failed, we found ourselves in a false position, unable to take advantage of the success with which our movements had been attended.[2]

Sir Robert Napier moved his division forward at once, and arrived at Palichao himself on 24 September. The 67th (Hampshires) left Tientsin on 27 September, escorting two batteries of the Royal Artillery, and covered the sixty miles to Palichao in record time. Brownlow's 8th Punjabis left five days earlier and marched seventy-six miles in three days, arriving at the camp on the 24th, where on 3 October they were joined by the various elements of the regiment which had been detached for guard duties. The 60th Rifles and a wing of the 99th (Wiltshires) arrived, and the last regiment to march in was the 1st Royal Scots, who arrived on the evening of 3 October. Bruce Tulloch remembered that march:

In the month of September, we were living comfortably in our camp at Tientsin, when we were aroused and ordered up at once. As usual, many men's boots gave out, but, barefooted or otherwise, every one pressed on, some men, and at times Officers also, carrying a rifle over each shoulder to help a weakly comrade. The miles were covered in a time which made the march a record and got the Regiment much kudos. The last day we had to leave the road, or rather track by the side of the river, and strike across the parklike country for the army, which was said to be somewhere between Tungchow and Peking. Guides we had none, and it began to look awkward when, near dusk, we came to a large canal with a broken bridge. This, however, we repaired somehow, and got the little transport we had safely over. Being by this time Acting Adjutant, – the real one was left ill at Tientsin, – I had as a charger a Tartar pony (which, by the way, was most useful during the march to some footsore elderly Officers). By means of my pony I got hold of some stray natives, and by their help we found the army, and marched in by moonlight. How we did enjoy a sleep that night![3]

The siege guns, which consisted of eight-inch guns and howitzers, with two thirty-two-pounders and three eight-inch mortars, had come up the river, and reached Tungchow on 29

September, together with 'A' Company of the Madras Sappers and Miners. Grant still had to wait for a large French convoy to arrive, and whilst doing so, pushed forward a party of the 60th Rifles to occupy a village on the north side of the canal, as an advanced post and a place where a depot could later be established. The French were expected by 3 October, but when by that date they had not arrived, Grant decided to advance.

In the meantime the mandarins of Tungchow had met Grant's requirements, and so the town was placed out of bounds to the troops; this was enforced by posting 400 Royal Marines at the north gate of the city, together with the same number of French infantry. However, there was trouble from the Chinese Coolie Corps, who could not resist plundering and murdering their fellow citizens. When six coolies entered Tungchow and tried to loot, the townsfolk killed two of them and handed the other four back to the Provost Marshal, who had them publicly flogged as an example. On another occasion, as Swinhoe relates,

Some officers out for a stroll, hearing loud shrieks in an adjoining field, caught three Coolies in the act of taking rude liberties with an unfortunate woman. The Officers laid hands on the miscreants and dragged them before the General. One was proved to be more criminally concerned than the others, and was condemned to be hanged, while his abettors in the crime were sentenced to 100 lashes each. At the time appointed for the execution, all the Coolies of the camp were assembled to witness it. The condemned man looked perfectly calm before his execution, and did not evince the slightest fear or trepidation, not even when the rope was being adjusted around his neck.[4]

There was also a certain amount of trouble on the lines of communication, with small parties of men being attacked by local villagers. Two Sikh sowars were fired upon five times when carrying letters, and a second party had to cut their way through a group of hostile and armed villagers. Colonel Urquhart, who was then at Matow, took a party of the 8th Punjabis and burnt the offending village, and this example had a salutary effect.

128

Discipline also had to be maintained amongst the troops. It is a reflection on the attitudes of the period that when a private soldier of the 99th Regiment (Wiltshires) was cheeky to the Provost Marshal, and received twenty-four lashes as a result, the troops considered it to be a huge joke.

Whilst the army was waiting at Palichao the Chinese continued trying to gain time. Grant reported on 22 September:

This morning letters came from the Emperor's brother to Lord Elgin and Baron Gros saying that he and another Chief Mandarin had been appointed by the Emperor in place of the former two, who, he stated, had been degraded in consequence of their having acted wrongly on the 18th September, the day of the first fight. And he stated that they were ready to enter into negotiations, but did not even allude to the Officers and men, of whom we have as yet heard nothing for certain. We understand, however, from the Mandarin who brought the letter, that upwards of thirty are now detained as prisoners in a court house at Peking, and we heard the same report, although the numbers were different, from a countryman, who had seen them on their way to Peking. I trust it may be true, and I do not doubt it, as they would not dare, I think, to injure any European. Lord Elgin has written to say he will have no communications with them, till the whole of the subjects of Her Majesty are given up, and he leaves the matter in the hands of the Commander in Chief. General Montauban and I had before written to say that if they were not given up, we should take Peking. I think, however, they are now so intimidated that they will do anything for the sake of peace.[1]

On the following day, 23 September, another letter came from the Chinese under a flag of truce, saying that as the prisoners had been captured as a result of their own intemperance, which resulted in their capture by the Chinese army after hostilities had commenced, they could not be released until peace had been established; they were, however, all in good health. In any case there could be no cause for possible alarm about a few British subjects who might be missing. Lord Elgin replied on the 25th that if the captives were not released by 29 September, hostilities would be renewed on the 30th.

. Answers came back on 27 September. The first letter was addressed to Lord Elgin saying that as the hostages had been taken on the orders of the previous Imperial Commissioners, they could not be released until the Allied army retired to Chang-kia-wan, but that orders had been given for them to be well cared for, and for their wounds to be treated. The second letter, to Baron Gros, the French diplomat, merely said that if the Allies marched on Peking, all the prisoners would be executed at once.

On 29 September yet another letter was addressed to Lord Elgin, apologising for the tone of the previous letters and saying that given the unsettled state of the populace in Peking, it would not be safe to send back the hostages. It suggested that Parkes might be used to negotiate between the parties; and a card was enclosed in Parkes's own handwriting, in both English and Chinese, making the same suggestion. There was also another note from Parkes asking for clothes for Loch and himself, and in the margin of this note was written in Hindustani 'By Order'. This was the first definite news that had been received from the prisoners and the first intimation that Loch was imprisoned with Parkes. It was also a clear indication that the other note had been sent under duress. The clothes were sent back with the flag of truce, together with a note in Hindustani, saying that the advance would begin in three days' time and asking where the prisoners were confined. Another letter from the prisoners stated that they were being held in a temple near one of the city gates.

Whilst the Allied army was encamped around Palichao, Grant sent out parties of cavalry each day to reconnoitre the Chinese positions. Probyn led one party to the north of Peking and established that the Chinese army was encamped in that area, and daily reconnaissances were made right up to the walls of Peking. Wolseley wrote:

Our cavalry was, indeed, of the utmost use to us throughout the whole campaign. Our two regiments and a half of cavalry there rendered most valuable service. With even that small force we were enabled to scour the country all around our camps to a great distance; and in action against the enemy, whose mounted force was considerable, they gave us the power of following up by rapid charges the effect produced at long ranges by our Armstrong guns. In our actions in the field, the Chinese suffered but very little from our infantry, our cavalry and artillery playing the principal parts, and inflicting almost all the loss which the enemy sustained.[2]

By 3 October there had been no satisfactory reply from the Chinese, and the reinforcements and the siege train had arrived. Grant ordered that the camp around Palichao be struck and the advance on Peking begun. The Yang-Liang canal was crossed by a bridge of boats and Grant established his headquarters in the village which had been occupied earlier by the 60th Rifles. The siege train, baggage and enough commissariat stores to supply the whole army up to 20 October were parked in the village. The French convoy arrived on 4 October and a general advance was ordered for the following day.

Early on the morning of the 5th, the army advanced in columns, with the French on the left and the British on the right. After a march of some four to five miles Peking could be seen in the distance, about six miles ahead. Grant and his staff surveyed the position from the top of a mound, and were making plans for the assault, when word came from General de Montauban asking for a postponement until the next day as his troops had marched further than the British and were tired. The troops had three days' salt meat in their haversacks but none of the baggage had come up, and so orders were given to bivouac on the spot. Meanwhile the cavalry reconnoitred ahead, attacked a Tartar camp, and reported the presence of a large force of Tartar cavalry. Both Probyn and Fane also found that any Chinese seen fled as soon as the Sikh sowars got anywhere near them.

On 6 October the advance was resumed with the cavalry leading. On gaining the limit of the previous day's reconnaissance, they found that the Tartar horse had retreated, leaving only a few pickets, which either made off to the flanks or retired rapidly. The Allied army halted for breakfast, and Grant and de Montauban surveyed the Chinese camp to the north of the city, where Sankolinsin was thought to be entrenched. A few Tartars could be seen keeping a watch on the Allied movements, but information concerning the whereabouts of the main Chinese army proved contradictory, some of the local people claiming that it was still within the main encampment, while others said that it had retreated north.

Grant reported to Sidney Herbert:

We halted for the night about 3 miles east of the north east angle of Peking, and the following morning [6 October] resumed our march in a north westerly direction, so as to pass along the northernmost face of the city, out of gunshot of the walls, and attack Sankolinsin's army, which was supposed to be encamped directly in our front. The country about here is not good for cavalry, from the great number of trees, villages and hollow roads; I accordingly despatched the Cavalry Brigade, with two six pounders with mounted detachments, with orders to advance on the road leading to the Emperor's palace at Yeun Ming Yeun, with a view to cutting off the retreat of the enemy in that direction. The French were on our left, whilst the English force moved along the outside of an old rampart, which runs parallel to the north face of the city. At this time we received information that the Chinese army was in full retreat, having commenced moving the night before. I therefore sent a message to General de Montauban, that I should advance at once to the Emperor's Palace.

On the road, however, we came across the rearguard, apparently of the enemy, with whom a few shots were exchanged, before they fled towards the city. As they appeared to be in considerable force in the suburb, I determined on halting on the great northern road, to prevent them moving out in that direction.[5]

Wolseley advanced with the infantry, who encountered little resistance other than small groups of Tartar cavalry hovering around their flanks. After three miles they occupied the area where Sankolinsin was believed to have had his camp and found it deserted. The French were nowhere to be seen. Grant therefore sent a message to General de Moutauban that he was going to march at once on the Summer Palace at Yuen Ming Yeun, because he had reason to think that that was the direction of the Chinese army's retreat.

Almost immediately after the despatch of that message our Advanced Guard came upon what seemed to be a large force of the enemy's cavalry, who seemed inclined to fight. The country was so very close that it was some time before we could bring our troops into line, and our advance was consequently slow. The enemy fell back before us, exchanging a few shots with our skirmishers. We soon found ourselves upon the main road, leading northwards from the Anting Gate, upon which we came in sight of a considerable cavalry force. Some skirmishing among the small villages close to the road ensued, and a few of the enemy were killed; but from the dense nature of the country, it was necessary to move with caution, and it was for a long time uncertain whether we were in presence of an army or of a detachment only. Our Allies had disappeared altogether; and, as evening was approaching, Sir Hope Grant determined upon halting there for the night, and sending out patrols the next morning to ascertain the exact position of our cavalry and that of our Allies. We bivouacked around a large temple.[2]

On the morning of 6 October Swinhoe had been called across to report to Grant, who

ordered me to attach myself to the Cavalry Brigade, who were well away to the right. I forthwith galloped in the direction I was told, and on opening a clump of trees found the Brigade halted, and awaiting the signal for general march. I reported myself to Brigadier Pattle, commanding, and rode by his side as the troopers advanced through the pretty wood-abounding country of this neighbourhood. The infantry were on our left at no great distance, and we rarely lost sight of them, except where a grove or a village intervened. At eleven, a halt was called, and a Staff Officer came riding across with orders for Brigadier Pattle to attend on the General. The halting place was close to a glaring red wall. Some unwholesome looking pools supplied the horses with ample water, and the troops refreshed themselves with a snack from their wallets, and a few whiffs from the ever cheering pipe.

The Brigadier soon returned to his Brigade with orders to proceed in a northerly direction for a few miles, and then to strike due west, and halt at any convenient place on the broad northern road leading to the city. In all probability the Tartars would retreat along the north road, when their encampment was attacked by the British and French infantry from the east; and thus an opportunity would be afforded to the Cavalry Brigade to intercept and cut off their retreat. The Cavalry were advancing to the north west, when the vedettes reported large bodies of Tartars moving north. The Brigade was halted, and a Squadron of Probyn's sent to observe the fugitives; but the Tartars sighted its approach, and made off.

We at last reached the broad road, and the Brigade were drawn up in a grove on an eminence, commanding open country on both right and left. The Brigadier sent me away with Captain Fane and a guard, to make enquiries as to the whereabouts of the Tartar camp. We had proceeded about two miles when we heard the report of muskets, and learned from a passing native that the Allies were already in the enemy's camp. With this intelligence we returned to the Brigadier, who determined to march towards the Allies. We arrived at a large temple, some three miles from Tishing Gate [of Peking], close to which we found the French halted, and making anxious enquiries after the British infantry. The Brigadier spoke with General Montauban, who said that he suspected Sir Hope Grant had moved on to the Summer Palace, where he had appointed the rendezvous at the close of the day. The French General then intimated his intention of advancing at once on the Palace, and begged that the Cavalry would move off his line of advance. The Brigadier thought it very odd that the French, who were only a short way on the left, should have lost sight of the British troops, and, thinking that they might have pushed on to the Summer Palace, he directed his Brigade thither also; but to avoid impeding the way of the French, we went some way up the north road before we struck across country for the Summer Palace in a north westerly direction.

The Brigadier resolved to move towards the French column. We found them on the road, and the Brigadier offered his co-operation in the capture of the Palace. To this the French General assented, and begged that he would keep well to the right round the walls of the gardens to cut off the retreating Tartars, while he attacked the central gate. The French then advanced while we moved round by the right. We were at the walls of the Palace, but we were completely closed in on our rear by a large populous village. The Brigadier, therefore, determined to defer entering the grounds until the morrow. As Colonel Walker and myself proceeded in advance we suddenly came across a party of some twenty mounted men, who were in a field raised above the level of the road. These made off as fast as they could go, and the Brigadier selected the ground they had left for the bivouac. The troops had orders to stand by their horses, and not to light fires until the moon rose at eleven.[4]

Grant, continuing his report, wrote:

The French anxious to join us in our advance, struck off to their right, and crossing the rear of our column, without either of us seeing the other, finished on the Palace without meeting any opposition, and occupied it about nightfall. The Cavalry Brigade had reached the Palace about two hours before this, and were there waiting for us to join them; on their way they saw a body of the enemy's cavalry, but were unable to come up with them.[5]

SOURCES

1 Royal Archives, Windsor Castle, RA VIC ADD MSS E/1, 2835.
2 Wolseley, Lieut-Colonel G. J., *Narrative of the War with China, 1860*, Longman, Green, Longman & Roberts, 1862.
3 Bruce Tulloch, Major-General Sir Alexander, *Recollections of Forty Years' Service*, Blackwood, 1903.
4 Swinhoe, R., *Narrative of the North China Campaign*, Smith Elder, 1861.
5 Royal Archives, Windsor Castle, RA VIC ADD MSS E/1, 2851.

13

On the morning of 7 October Grant ordered that a salvo of twenty-one guns be fired from the bivouac where the infantry had encamped amongst the old Chinese emplacements. This would indicate their position to the French and to the Cavalry Brigade. The cavalry heard the sound of the firing and at first thought that the attack on Peking had commenced, but when it became clear that the twenty-one guns were being fired at regular intervals, it was surmised that either the city had surrendered and a royal salute was being fired in celebration, or that this was to warn the cavalry of the location of the infantry. A patrol under Lieutenant-Colonel Wolseley soon made contact with the Cavalry Brigade, and later Grant, accompanied by Lord Elgin, rode across to see Brigadier Pattle and to speak with General de Montauban.

Brigadier Pattle, with Swinhoe as interpreter and two other officers, had already paid a visit to the French, who on reaching the Palace the night before had encountered only feeble resistance from some two dozen poorly equipped eunuchs, who were quickly dealt with. General de Montauban placed a guard on the main gate and camped his force outside under some trees. He reserved a large open space for the Cavalry Brigade, which he expected to join him after they returned from chasing the Tartar cavalry. When the cavalry failed to materialise, however, the French soldiers became nervous. Twice during the night they panicked and their officers had great difficulty in restoring calm and control. General de Montauban was relieved to see Pattle, and told him that he had forbidden his troops from entering the Palace or from any looting, but he said that he had had a few of the best things set aside to be presented to the French Emperor and to Queen Victoria.

De Montauban offered to show Pattle and his party over the Palace grounds, and the British were amazed to see with what speed the accompanying French officers started to fill their pockets with anything of value, when all the while de Montauban kept on insisting that he had forbidden any looting and that nothing was to be touched until Grant arrived. As the party returned to the French camp, an officer came up to de Montauban and told him that a Chinese peasant had been caught stealing a pair of shoes. The offender was brought before the General, who proceeded to beat him with his cane. De Montauban and Pattle then went off to breakfast, and the French officers showed the rest of the British party some of the treasures which they had managed to acquire; these included strings of pearls, pencil cases set with diamonds, and watches set with pearls.

Grant soon arrived with his staff, shortly afterwards followed by Lord Elgin. As they walked about the extensive grounds, the French continued their depredations, and a French officer commented that 'General Montauban's prohibition places us quite in a false position. The General says you must not loot, and yet he allows it to take place before his own eyes.' Lord Elgin was deeply shocked and said, 'I would like a great many things that the Palace contains, but I am not a thief.'[1] Wolseley took a more relaxed view:

Soldiers are nothing more than grown-up schoolboys. The wild moments of enjoyment passed in the pillage of a place live long in a soldier's memory. Although, perhaps, they did not gain sixpence by it, still they talk of such for years afterwards with pleasure. Such a time forms so marked a contrast with the ordinary routine of existence passed under the tight hand of discipline, that it becomes a remarkable event in life and is remembered accordingly. When looting is once commenced by an army it is no easy matter to stop it. At such times human nature breaks down the ordinary trammels which discipline imposes, and the consequences are most demoralising to the very best constituted army.[2]

The ground around the French camp was covered with silks and clothing of all kinds, whilst the men ran hither and thither in search of further plunder, most of them, according to the practice usual with soldiers upon such occasions, being decked out in the most ridiculous looking costumes they could find, of which there was no lack. I stood by whilst one of the regiments was supposed to be parading; but although their fall-in was sounded over and over again, I do not believe there was an average of ten men a company present . . . Three days afterwards when the French moved into their position before Peking, they seemed to have regained their discipline, and their men were as steady under arms as if nothing had occurred to disturb the ordinary routine of their lives.[2]

The British infantry were kept confined to their camp, but some of the officers managed to pay visits to the Summer Palace. Bruce Tulloch asked Sir John Michel if he might be allowed to pay a visit and the General agreed that up to one third of the officers might be away at any one time.

'But remember,' he said, 'there must be no looting.' In a few minutes we all drew lots who were to go. I was one of the lucky ones, and at once was away on my Tartar pony, riding hard towards a column of smoke in the far distance, having heard part of the Palace was on fire. I got eventually to the outer gate, where I noticed some men, quite off their heads with the excitement of looting a palace, and for no apparent reason tearing down grand embroideries. I saw one man send the butt of his rifle through a huge mirror, possibly because the reflection of his own unwashed and ugly mug did not please him. With the feeling of a boy suddenly told to take what he likes in a pastry-cook's shop, I was puzzled where to begin. I, knowing the great value of jade, made a collection that probably has rarely been seen. I soon had my prize on the pony, and with both arms around the pieces, I started to return to camp. In a narrow way I met some Sikh Cavalry; they opened their ranks to let me pass, their eyes glittering at the sight of my load. As I passed them I sung out [in Hindustani] 'Be quick or it will all be gone'. With a shout they put spurs to their horses, and I trust they got all they expected.[3]

Whilst the French were busy, only a few of the British officers managed to visit the Summer Palace, and most of those were from the staff. The men of the infantry divisions were confined to camp, and it was only some of the Sikhs and dragoons of the Cavalry Brigade who were able to acquire some plunder, as that brigade spent another night in the immediate vicinity of the Summer Palace before moving to the British camp before the Tishing Gate. Several of Probyn's men were seen carrying away pony-loads of valuable Chinese silks, and sixty years later one of Probyn's pensioners, Kot-Daffadar Gurdit Singh, admitted that he had made more than Rs500 as a result of the loot he had taken from the Summer Palace.[4]

This caused a great deal of dissatisfaction among the British troops generally, and Grant took immediate action. Bruce Tulloch remembered:

That evening a hateful order came out. 'The Commander in Chief expects that all Officers who may have got anything out of the Summer Palace will give up what they may have taken to the Prize Committee, to be sold at auction for the benefit of the Army.' Considering the value of my collection the order was crushing; but in every atom of it went. The Prize Committee, seeing how much I had given up, gave me afterwards a few small pieces back. Notwithstanding the order, a friend came to me the following morning with a good sized parcel of pearls to exchange for a small piece of my jade. On my informing him that I had given it all to the Prize Committee, there came from the very bottom of his heart, 'Eh, ye big fule!'[3]

A certain amount of gold in ingots had been discovered in a room of the Summer Palace. A guard was placed on it and the gold shared out between the French and the British. The British share was placed with the Prize Committee, and this together with the articles handed in was put up for auction. Grant ordered that one third of the proceeds be awarded to the officers and two thirds to the other ranks. Grant and the two divisional generals renounced all claim to their share of the prize money and the final share out resulted in each private soldier receiving £4, with the amount increasing in proportion to rank. This firm action helped to quell the grumbling, although as the French were allowed to keep their gains, and as the 1st Division felt that the loot acquired by the officers of the 2nd Division was not subjected to such strict rules of surrender as had been imposed on them, the grumbling never completely died away.

Several regiments managed to put aside trophies which still grace their messes and regimental museums today. A silver ingot is displayed in the Museum of 1st The Queen's Dragoon Guards; a very large and beautiful vase, taken by the Colonel of the 2nd Queen's, is now in the National Army Museum; the 99th (Wiltshires) Regiment brought back five magnificent vases which are still the property of the Duke of Edinburgh's Royal Regiment. Captain Hart Dunne of the 99th returned to England with a small Chinese sleeve dog, which was presented to Queen Victoria. It was the first Pekinese to enter Britain, and was appropriately named 'Looty'.[5]

Grant told the Duke of Cambridge:

It is sad, sad indeed. That the Chinese have received severe retribution there is little doubt, and the celebrated palace of the Emperor, his summer residence, has been taken by the French, and turned inside out. I was much struck with the appearance of this magnificent palace, full of beautiful pieces of water and fine buildings and pagodas.[6]

On 7 October a letter was received from the Chinese, countersigned by Parkes, saying that all the hostages would be returned on the 8th. This letter was dated 6 October, but the Chinese bearer, setting out on that day, had turned back to Peking when he came into contact with the Allied army on the march, and so did not deliver his missive until the 7th. A verbal reply was sent back that Mr Wade would meet the Chinese outside the city walls at four o'clock. He reported on the 8th, 'I went yesterday evening at five o'clock to a temple outside the Tishing Gate to meet Hungki, the deputy of the Prince of Kung, and I communicated to him the decision at which Your Excellency and General de Montauban had arrived.' This informed the Chinese that they must honour the treaties already entered into, including the recent agreement made at Tientsin, and that the prisoners must be returned immediately. Failure to comply would cause the capital city of Peking to be stormed, 'in order to show to those who break faith and do injury to others, that sooner or later their offence will be punished'. Once the prisoners were handed back, a date could be set for the signing of the Convention, but before 'Their Excellencies enter Peking, a Gate of the capital will have to be occupied by an escort detached from both armies, and the Chinese troops will be then required to fall back for the time being.' Wade reported, 'Beyond the rendition of the prisoners, Hungki would speak authoritatively upon nothing. I returned to Headquarters.'[7]

Next day, 8 October, Bruce Tulloch

Happened to walk a little way in front of our bivouac towards Peking, when I met a European riding towards me. As he came close I saw by the drawn and almost parchment colour of his face that he must have had some terrible suffering, and it was not until he spoke that I recognised Mr Parkes, whom I had known well at Canton. He and Loch had only a few minutes before been released by the Chinese.[3]

The Chinese had also released Sowar Nihal Singh of Probyn's Horse, who had been carrying their flag of truce, as well as a French officer, de Lauture, and four French soldiers. Grant reported that

The Chinese declare that these are all of the prisoners who were in Peking, the rest having been conveyed some distance into the interior. They have, however, been sent for, and will be given up in the course of a few days.[8]

Parkes and Loch were fortunate, for when the Chinese heard the British artillery firing their twenty-one guns, they supposed that an assault upon the capital had begun, and orders were sent to execute the prisoners at once. These orders arrived at the prison just fifteen minutes after Parkes and Loch had been released. Grant reported:

Messrs Parkes and Loch have given the following account of their capture; when Captain Brabazon and Mr Loch left the Army on the 18th September to recall Mr Parkes's party, they proceeded at once to Tungchow, where they experienced a short delay in collecting them all together, and then set out to return. On arriving within a few hundred yards of the centre of the Chinese position, where they had left Colonel Walker, they heard firing commence, and immediately their passage was barred by a large body of cavalry and infantry, the Commander of whom informed them that firing having commenced, he could not permit them to pass without Sankolinsin's orders. Considering that it would be almost impossible to cut their way through the large bodies which surrounded them, they decided on trusting to the flag of truce which they carried.

Accordingly Messrs Parkes and Loch, accompanied by one Sikh orderly with a white flag, quitted the rest of the party to go and speak with Sankolinsin; whilst there, they were surrounded and made prisoners, by order of Sankolinsin himself, and sent into Peking, when for several days they were treated with great severity. On the 29th September they were removed from the jail, and have been since treated in a proper manner. The rest of the party they know nothing of, beyond having heard Sankolinsin, at the time of their capture, order the remainder to be seized also, and sent back to Tungchow. The five Frenchmen given up were taken prisoners in Tungchow, whilst walking about the streets, and ignorant of what was going on.

Mr Parkes states that at first they were tied with their hands behind their backs, and taken up in a cart to Peking, where they were placed in irons and confined in the common prison.[8]

On 12 October eight more sowars and one French soldier were released and came into the Allied camp. Grant wrote:

I am sad and sorry to inform you that the poor prisoners, nine of whom were given up to us last night, have been shamefully treated. Lieutenant Anderson, who commanded the escort, died after nine days; his hands and feet were tied so tightly behind his back that it produced mortification. Mr De Norman, Attaché to Mr Bruce, died from bad usage after seventeen days, and the eight Sowars who have come in are more or less injured, but I trust will all recover. The ninth was a Frenchman. Five more, all that remain are expected in today, and if they return in time, I shall inform you of their names. I trust Captain Brabazon and Mr Bowlby may be amongst this number. The remainder have either died or were killed on the 18th September in the firing at the commencement, and several, as far as I understand, Sikhs I presume, would not eat what was prepared for them, and died of starvation.[8]

On 14 October the last two surviving prisoners, both Sikh sowars, were returned, but one of these had been so badly treated that he died that evening. These nineteen survivors were all that remained alive out of the twenty-six British and thirteen French who were seized by the Chinese, most of them whilst under the protection of a flag of truce. Out of the eighteen men of Fane's Horse who had been captured, eight died in captivity. As the details of their imprisonment started to emerge, the temper of the Allied troops against the Chinese rose.

When Parkes and Loch with Sowar Nihal Singh were dragged from their horses and taken before Sankolinsin, they were forcibly held down and made to kowtow before the Chinese General, with their faces being rubbed in the dirt. They were then bullied to tell Sankolinsin the dispositions of the Allied troops. When they refused he ordered that they be taken back to Chang-kia-wan. Sowar Nihal Singh of Probyn's Horse, a gallant soldier, had been most unwilling to surrender; as the Chinese closed in on the three, he brought his lance down to the charge and prepared to fight. When they had been taken, he said to Parkes, 'Oh, Sahib, if we had only charged, it would have been alright, and we should have escaped.' As they were being led away Loch told him to keep up his spirits and not to be afraid; Nihal Singh replied, 'I do not fear. If I don't die today, I may tomorrow, and I am past sixty; and am I not with you? I do not fear.' His courage during his confinement was outstanding; on his return his hands were crippled from the tightness of the cords binding his wrists, and the sores took months to heal. Major Probyn promoted him on the spot to the rank of daffadar, and he was awarded £100 for his bravery.[4]

The rest of Parkes's escort had been left waiting on the road near Chang-kia-wan, when Parkes and Loch went to meet Sankolinsin. The escort did not know what was happening to Parkes, and the longer they waited for his return the number of Chinese gathering around them increased. As Wolseley commented:

Of all the horrible positions in which I can fancy an Officer being placed, I think that of Messrs Brabazon and Anderson [in command of the escort] must have been the worst. All their subsequent ill-treatment must have been insignificant, when compared with the moments of uncertainty which they passed whilst awaiting in vain for the return of Mr Parkes. There cannot be much doubt that, if the escort had charged, most of them would have reached our Army safely. The Sowars were all picked men and well mounted, and none, who knew either of the two Officers with the party, imagine, I am sure, that they were men who would have preferred taking the chances of imprisonment to that of a hand to hand encounter.

They became hemmed in on all sides closely. They were then really prisoners and had to give up their arms, after which they were ordered to dismount, but had their horses subsequently given back to them. They were conducted to the rear, and lodged for the night in a joss house. The next morning they were ordered to mount again, and were taken to the capital. Whilst on the road Captain Brabazon and the Abbé de Luc left them, saying they were going back to our camp to make arrangements for the release of all the party. That was the last ever seen of them by any of our people. All the information subsequently gleaned from Chinese sources tends to prove that both were beheaded on the 21st September during the action fought upon that day.[2]

The French had succeeded in wounding the Chinese General Pao at the Palichao bridge, and apparently he had ordered the execution of Brabazon and de Luc in revenge. Two headless bodies were seen floating in the Yang-Liang canal, but were thought at the time to be those of fair-skinned Tartars.

On arrival in Peking the prisoners were paraded through the streets and then taken to the Summer Palace, where they were confined six to a tent, with the Europeans and Sikhs separated. After two hours the Chinese brought out first the British, then the French and finally the Sikhs. As they were brought out they were thrown down onto their faces, and their hands and feet were tied together behind them; the British and the French were tied with double strands and the Sikhs with single. The ropes were pulled as tight as possible, and then soaked in water in order to shrink them further. The men were then placed in a kneeling position and kicked over onto their backs. If they tried to move they were beaten and forced back so that all their weight rested on their bound hands, which, with the circulation cut off, soon became swollen and black. They were then carried into a courtyard, with a Chinese soldier allotted to each prisoner, where they were left exposed to the sun and rain for three days and nights without any food or water. Crowds of Chinese came to stare at them and watch their suffering, and if they moved or asked for anything they were kicked and beaten. When they pleaded for food, dirt was forced into their mouths and they were kicked about the head. At the end of the third day of their captivity a little food was handed out, and irons were put on their hands, feet and necks.

On the second day in the Summer Palace, Lieutenant Anderson became delirious. His hands were badly swollen and black, and as they deadened his fingers and nails burst, and worms and maggots collected in a festering mass about his hands and wrists. On the afternoon of the fourth day the prisoners were split into four parties and carried away in carts to four hill forts between twenty and forty miles from Peking. The first party consisted of Lieutenant Anderson, Mr De Norman, a daffadar and four Sikh sowars; the second, three Frenchmen and five Sikhs; the third, Mr Bowlby, a French officer, Private Phipps of the King's Dragoon Guards, and four Sikhs; the last, three Frenchmen and four Sikhs. On reaching the forts, they were placed in cages and loaded with chains. Lieutenant Anderson died on the ninth day, and his body was left lying among the other prisoners in their cage for three days before being removed. But on the evening of Anderson's death, the ropes were removed from the wrists and feet of all the other prisoners in that first party. On the fourteenth day a Sikh sowar died to be followed by de Norman on the seventeenth day; the daffadar and three sowars survived and were among those who were returned, but their wrists and ankles were a mass of sores and their fingers had contracted and become useless.

In the second party a Frenchman died on the way to the fort, and another died the day after arrival. The survivors fared better than the other parties, for the mandarin at the fort had their bonds and irons removed and their wounds washed and tended, so that the remaining Frenchman and the five Sikh sowars all returned. The third party were not so fortunate; of the Europeans only Private Phipps of the King's Dragoon Guards spoke a little Hindustani, and the Sikh sowars spoke no English. On their release Sowars Bughel Singh and Khan Singh of Fane's Horse testified:

Another cart was with us containing Daffadar Mahomed Bux, a French Officer, very tall and stout, with a brown beard, and a Dragoon named Pisa [Phipps]. We were taken into the fort, and for three days were out in the open air in the cold. They then pulled us into an old kitchen and kept us there for three or four days. Mr Bowlby died the second day after we arrived. The next day the Frenchman died. Two days after this Jawalla Singh died. Four days afterwards, Phipps, King's Dragoon Guards died; for ten days he encouraged us in every way he could. Mahomed Bux, Daffadar, died ten days ago; he remained very well till then, and abused the Chinese for bringing him pig to eat. I should have died had not my chains been taken off.[9, 10]

Wolseley commented on Private Phipps's example:

Up to the day of his death, he never lost heart, and, always endeavoured to cheer up those about him when any complained or bemoaned their cruel fate. Even to his last moment of consciousness he tried to encourage them with words of hope and comfort. All honour be to his memory: he was brave when hundreds of brave men would have lost heart. Nothing except the very highest order of courage, both mental and bodily, will sustain a man through the miseries of such a barbarous imprisonment and cruel torture as that which Private Phipps underwent patiently, his resolute spirit living within him up to the very last moments of his existence.[2]

SOURCES

1 Swinhoe, R., *Narrative of the North China Campaign*, Smith Elder, 1861.
2 Wolseley, Lieut-Colonel G. J., *Narrative of the War with China, 1860*, Longman, Green, Longman & Roberts, 1862.
3 Bruce Tulloch, Major-General Sir Alexander, *Recollections of Forty Years' Service*, Blackwood, 1903.
4 Maxwell, Captain E. L., *History of the 11th King Edward's Own Lancers*, A. C. Curtis, 1914.
5 Kenrick, Colonel N. C. E., *The Story of the Wiltshire Regiment*, Gale & Polden, 1963.
6 Royal Archives, Windsor Castle, RA VIC ADD MSS E/1, 2858.
7 Royal Archives, Windsor Castle, RA VIC ADD MSS E/1, 2849.
8 Royal Archives, Windsor Castle, RA VIC ADD MSS E/1, 2851.
9 Royal Archives, Windsor Castle, RA VIC ADD MSS E/1, 2859.
10 Bowlby, C. C., *An Account of the Last Mission and Death of Thomas William Bowlby*, private circulation, 1906.

14

On 9 October the French left their camp at the Summer Palace and formed up on the left of the British line opposite the walls of Peking, with the Anting Gate opposite the centre of the Allied army. Grant needed to bring the hostilities to a speedy conclusion before the harsh Chinese winter set in and the Pei-ho froze over, making an already difficult supply situation impossible. Lord Elgin had suggested that the soldiers might winter in Peking, but Grant refused to countenance this and insisted that the army must be back in Tientsin by the start of November. An ultimatum was sent to the Chinese demanding the surrender of the Anting Gate by midday on 13 October, failing which Peking would be subjected to bombardment.

On 9 October Grant wrote to say that 'The heavy guns will arrive from Tungchow today, so that the Chinese will see that we are prepared to enforce our demands in the event of their deceiving us.'[1] In fact there was a good deal of bluff behind these moves, because the walls of Peking were some forty feet high and sixty feet thick, and it was doubtful whether the Allied artillery was adequate to breach them in the time available. In addition, although the Chinese army had been defeated, it was still a coherent force lying somewhere to the north of the city and possibly capable of dislocating the Allied plans.

Grant and de Montauban made a reconnaissance of the northern walls and decided to place their breaching batteries some six hundred yards to the right of the Anting Gate. As the officers rode up to the edge of the ditch surrounding the city walls, the Chinese manning them held up white flags, but did not fire. Later Bruce Tulloch was not so lucky. The Royal Scots were brought up

to dig trenches and prepare the wall enclosing our camp for bringing a rifle fire on the city wall. The guns were parked close to us, and then placed in battery behind the wall, through which embrasures covered by mantlets were cut. The Regiment worked all night, and in the morning, being Adjutant, I went into the trench to see how it was getting on. We were only two hundred yards from the wall when a desire came on me to examine it more closely, so I walked out of the trench across the open right up to the wall. As soon as I got there a perfect shower of heavy stones came all around me: how it was I escaped I do not know. Our men in the trench shouted to me to come back, but I thought it undignified to return at a greater pace than I went. Before returning I shook my fist at the enemy, which, as a Chinaman can enjoy a joke more than most people, doubtless amused my friends on the wall sixty feet above my head.[2]

The heavy guns were placed inside a temple, just outside the city, which was itself surrounded by a high wall. The four eight-inch guns and two Armstrong twelve-pounders, together with the mortars, were to make the breach and widen it, whilst two more Armstrongs were to fire down the road leading to the Anting Gate, with another two in reserve. In addition a battery of nine-pounders was available for counter-battery work. The guns were on wooden platforms, with magazines stored in lean-tos against the wall of the temple. The French had no heavy guns but proposed to use their field batteries, and these were installed to the left of the British batteries and nearer to the city wall. In front of the batteries trenches were dug to accommodate riflemen, who could pick off any Chinese showing their heads above the city walls.

The Chinese had been told that if the Anting Gate was not surrendered by noon on 13 October, the city of Peking would be taken by storm. All the batteries were ready and the infantry moved up during the night of the 12th; the 1st Royal Scots were in and around the breaching batteries in the temple, the 67th Regiment (Hampshires) formed the storming party, with the 8th Punjabis in support. The Chinese havered and tried to avoid surrendering the city, but Parkes was insistent. Bruce Tulloch described those few minutes before midday:

At a quarter to twelve there was no sign of surrender: the guns were loaded and the mantlets cleared away, the Regiment [1st Royal

Scots] manning the prepared position along the top of our wall. The Chiefs with watches in their hands were waiting for the eventful moment, which had almost arrived, when the Chinese surrendered, and threw open the huge gate. Our men and the French rushed in, secured the great bastion-like masonry works which enclosed the double gates, and Peking was ours.[2]

Both the 67th (Hampshires) and the 8th Punjabis claimed to be the first into the gate. The Hampshire's Regimental History relates: 'The 67th were ready to lead the assaulting column when, just before the Allies' ultimatum expired, the Chinese capitulated, whereupon the 67th, instead of storming the gate, took possession of it peacefully.'[3] The 8th Punjabis account says: 'As the siege guns were on the point of opening fire, the Anting Gate was surrendered, and the Regiment doubled in and occupied it, being the first Corps, French or English, to enter Peking and to plant the British colours on its walls.'[4] Swinhoe continues:

They marched a few yards into the city, driving the dense crowd before them, and then took possession of the Gate, quartering themselves on the right side. The French then marched in, drums beating and colours flying, and pushing some distance farther along the broad road, returned and established themselves on the left side of the gate-top. A rope was then stretched across the road to keep the crowd back, and sentries posted, and entrance for the time strictly forbidden.[5]

The Allies occupied the walls of the city from the Anting to the Tishing Gates, and the Royal Engineers fortified positions in case of attack from the city, with field guns mounted on the walls to cover all the main approaches. That evening Grant reported, 'One of the Gates of Peking has been given up to us unconditionally, and the flags of the two nations are now flying from the top of it.'[6]

The main difficulty was not caused by any hostile intentions on the part of the Chinese, but more by sheer curiosity. Wolseley wrote:

As soon as our troops had taken up their position in the Anting gate, the crowds of people that swarmed in from all quarters of the city to gaze at us exceeded anything that I had ever previously witnessed: a perfect sea of heads stretched away up the broad street as far as we could see. The moving to and fro of these people caused such clouds of dust to arise, that, in some directions, the city was so enveloped by it that nothing was to be seen. The Chinese guard, aided by a number of the city police, had much difficulty in keeping back the dense masses, which, swaying to and fro, kept pressing down towards the gate.

On 14 October Swinhoe

was out with Colonel Wolseley and a party of the Cavalry on a survey of the west wall. We had just fallen in with a company of some twenty Tartar troopers, who fled before us, when we encountered a party with five carts, each cart bearing a coffin. On the head of each coffin was pasted a piece of paper, inscribed, in Chinese characters, with the name of the deceased person it contained. The one marked, 'Ponepe, died of disease on the 25th September,' referred to Mr Bowlby, the ill-fated Correspondent of The Times. By the 17th all the bodies were returned; they were found to be in such a fearful state of decomposition that not a feature was recognisable, and it was only by the tattered garments that the doctors made them out to be the remains of Mr De Norman, Lieutenant Anderson of Fane's Horse; Private John Phipps, King's Dragoon Guards, and eight Sikhs.[5]

Bowlby's son noted that 'quicklime had destroyed their features, but we recognised them by their clothes'.[8] The French also were handed back the bodies of most of their missing men. Grant reported:

The Chinese have sent in the bodies of twenty-one in coffins, and amongst the number have been recognised those belonging to Lieutenant Anderson, Mr de Norman, Mr Bowlby, and the man from the King's Dragoon Guards, named Phipps, who was one of the escort, and whose conduct, I understand from the others, was most admirable throughout, encouraging and keeping up the spirits of the other prisoners.[9]

Grant was determined to bury the dead prisoners with full military honours in order to impress upon the Chinese the regard felt for them, and the great value placed upon their lives. The Russian Minister in Peking, Count Ignatieff, offered the use of the Russian Cemetery, and on 17 October the band of the 60th Rifles, with a troop of the King's Dragoon Guards and a troop of Fane's Horse, together with marching detachments of an officer and twenty men from each infantry regiment, led the procession of gun carriages, each one bearing a coffin, to the Russian Cemetery near to the Anting Gate. Grant and Elgin, with as many officers as could be spared from their duties, as well as a large number of French officers, all in full uniform, attended the funerals. The attachés from the Russian Embassy were also present. The service was conducted by the chaplain, the Revd McGhee. A few days later the dead French were buried in the Jesuit Cemetery to the west of the city, and this funeral was again attended by Grant and many British officers. Grant and the other senior British officers were invited to sprinkle holy water over the graves, and this offer apparently stirred Grant's Scottish prejudices; but when he saw Sir Robert Napier, 'an excellent man', accepting, he followed his example. The dead Sikhs were ceremoniously cremated, according to Sikh custom.

Tempers in the Allied army were running high at the treatment meted out to the prisoners, and at what was considered to be Chinese duplicity and bad faith. The Allies had given their word that Peking would be spared if the city were surrendered, and so Lord Elgin determined to set an example by burning the Summer Palace, where the ill-treatment of the prisoners had started. This move was popular with the British but, strangely enough, was opposed by the French on the grounds that it was destruction for the sake of destruction, and could have a bad effect upon world opinion. They declined to take part, and then suggested that if the Chinese remained difficult the Imperial Palace in Peking itself should be destroyed.

On 18 October, the 1st Division under General Sir John Michel, together with the King's Dragoon Guards, marched from Peking to the Summer Palace. Separate buildings were allotted to different companies for destruction. The 15th Punjabis found large quantities of gold and one of their officers managed to acquire some £9,000 worth. Captain (later General) Gordon, RE wrote home:

Owing to the ill-treatment the prisoners experienced at the Summer Palace the General ordered it to be destroyed, and stuck up proclamations to say why it was ordered. We accordingly went out, and after pillaging it burned the whole place, destroying in a Vandal like manner most valuable property which could not be replaced for four millions. Quantities of gold ornaments were burned, considered as brass. It was wretchedly demoralising for an Army. Everybody was wild for plunder. You would scarcely conceive the magnificence of this residence, or the tremendous devastation the French have committed. The French have smashed everything in the most wanton manner. It was a scene of utter destruction which passes my description.[10]

Swinhoe saw

a dense column of smoke rising to the sky, and as the day waned the column increased in magnitude, and grew denser and denser, wafting in the shape of a large cloud over Peking, and having the semblance of a fearful thunderstorm impending. As we approached the Palace the crackling and rushing noise of fire was appalling, and the sun shining through the masses of smoke gave a sickly hue to every plant and tree, and the red flame gleaming on the faces of the troops engaged made them appear like demons glorying in the destruction. The day was not sufficient to accomplish the work, so the troops had to bivouac out, and finish their work on the morrow. Before sunset on the 19th, every place had been fired, and the troops were marched back to camp.[5]

Wolseley thought that

The destruction of the Palace appears to have struck the Peking authorities with awe. It was the stamp which gave an unmistakable reality to our work of vengeance, proving that Lord Elgin's last letter was no idle threat, and warning them of what they might expect in the capital itself, unless they accepted our proferred terms. By the evening of the 19th the Summer Palaces had ceased to exist, leaving them a dreary waste of ruined nothings.[7]

Sidney Herbert, writing to Queen Victoria, enclosed

some letters received this day from Sir Hope Grant. Your Majesty will see from the correspondence with General de Montauban that the French, having appropriated the lion's share in the plunder of the Palace, affected a certain prudery as to burning it, as a retribution for the cruel and treacherous treatment of the unhappy priosners. Major

Anson, who brought the despatches, says that the Treaty would never have been obtained had the Summer Palace not been burned, but that its destruction greatly alarmed them, and gave additional force to the threat to destroy the Palaces in Peking.[11]

The negotiations with the Chinese were now pushed forward. 300,000 taels of compensation money were handed over on the evening of 22 October, and it was proposed to sign the Convention on the following day, but as copies of the Treaty had to be made in both English and Chinese, the signing was postponed until the 24th. Snow had already fallen on the hills surrounding Peking and there were rumours of double dealing and foul play by the Chinese negotiators, as well as the alleged approach of the Chinese army, who were said to be establishing a large camp to the west of Peking. Grant was now in a hurry to get back to Tientsin before the winter set in, and was in no mood to have further delays imposed by Chinese methods of diplomacy. He wrote to the Duke of Cambridge:

We have taken from the Government upwards of 800 guns, and the prestige of the [Chinese] Empire is broken up, an English and French flag flying at the summit of one of the Gates of the city. The weather still continues beautiful and most healthy. I trust Lord Elgin will now be enabled to make a treaty. Prince Kung has several times stated that he is ready to agree to anything, but at present he is in too great a fright to enter the town.[5]

Lord Elgin began to apply diplomatic pressure, and reminded the Chinese that any further delay would result in the destruction of the Imperial Palaces in Peking, the cutting off of customs revenue at Canton, the withdrawal of Allied soldiers from Shanghai, and the blockade of the Pei-ho river up which rice and revenue flowed to the Imperial Government from the rest of China.

At the same time Grant took certain precautions: each day the cavalry went out and scoured the area around Peking, and on 22 October a party led by Major Probyn came across an entrenched position just to the west of the city, which was occupied by a considerable force of Tartars. As the cavalry approached the Tartars turned out, and Probyn brought back the mandarin in charge to the Allied camp for questioning.

Grant also had more guns placed on the wall by the Tishing Gate, ready to open fire on the city if necessary, and Brownlow's Punjabis were warned to be ready to attack the Imperial Palace if occasion demanded.

The signing was fixed for the afternoon of the 24th, and because there had been rumours that the Hall of Audience, where the ceremony was to take place, might have been mined, Lieutenant-Colonel Wolseley and an officer of the Quartermaster General's department, accompanied by Parkes and Wade, the officials entrusted with arranging the details for the signing, paid a visit to check the building on the evening of the 23rd. Before the procession set out on the 24th, Sir Robert Napier positioned the infantry of the 2nd Division along the line of march, so that every possible approach to the Hall was covered.

At 3 p.m. on the 24th the Allied procession entered the Anting Gate. It was led by a detachment of fifty cavalry, drawn from the King's Dragoon Guards, Probyn's and Fane's Horse, followed by two hundred men drawn from the various infantry regiments. The regimental bands of the 60th Rifles and the 67th (Hampshires) led the infantry detachments and played alternately on the march. The leading infantry detachments were followed by officers on foot, and then the mounted officers, culminating in Sir Hope Grant surrounded by his staff. This military show of strength gave place to Lord Elgin seated in a green sedan chair, which was carried by sixteen coolies in scarlet livery. The procession ended with another escort of fifty cavalry and two hundred infantry. As the procession passed through the Anting Gate, the French guard turned out and saluted, with their band playing 'God Save The Queen'.

The Hall of Audience lay on the south side of the city, and so the procession marched right through the centre of Peking for a distance of three miles. On arrival a guard of honour, found from the 99th Regiment (Wiltshires) with their colours, presented arms. The Convention was signed by the Prince of

Kung for the Chinese, and by Lord Elgin for the Allies. The procession then returned to the Allied camp. On the following day, 25 October, the French engaged in a similar exercise and signed their agreement with the Chinese.

Wolseley had noticed that the weather had changed perceptibly after 10 October, with the nights becoming bitterly cold, but fortunately a supply of warm clothing and blankets arrived for the troops on the 21st. The 60th Rifles suffered most from sickness, although their sick rate never exceeded five per cent of their strength, and this was attributed to the fact that so many of their men were young soldiers. The 60th also lost six of their riflemen, who went out unarmed to scour the ruins of the Summer Palace and were never seen again.[5, 7]

Grant started to move the troops back to Peking, even before the Convention had been signed; the siege train with the heavy guns left for Tientsin on 22 October and the heavy stores and the sick were moved by carts to Tungchow, where they were ferried by boat to Tientsin. On 1 November de Montauban left with the French contingent, except for one infantry battalion which stayed behind as guard to Baron Gros. Mr Bruce, who was to be the new British Ambassador, arrived at Peking on 7 November, but as there was no suitable accommodation for him or for M. de Bourboulon, the French Ambassador, it was agreed that they would live for the time being at Tientsin.

On 7 November Sir Robert Napier led the 2nd Division out of Peking on their march to Tientsin, and the next day Sir Hope Grant followed with Sir John Michel's 1st Division. As the troops marched, a flotilla of boats on the Pei-ho river kept pace with them to pick up any sick or casualties. The King's Dragoon Guards of the Cavalry Brigade set out for Tientsin on 7 November, with Probyn's and Fane's Horse staying until the 9th. The rearguard consisted of the 60th Rifles and the 15th Punjabis with Barry's battery of the Royal Artillery.

As the troops marched back to Tientsin, the detachment of the 60th Rifles guarding the advanced depot near the Palichao bridge was picked up, as were the Royal Marines left at Tungchow. At Chang-kia-wan the squadron of Fane's Horse left there joined the column, and on arrival at Hosiwu the garrison comprising the 31st Regiment (East Surrey) was collected. However, as the approaches to Tientsin were becoming overcrowded with troops and stores from the retiring army, the 15th Punjabis, Fane's Horse and Barry's battery of the Royal Artillery from the rearguard had to wait for some days at Hosiwu until the congestion at Tientsin was cleared.

Bruce Tulloch described the march from Peking:

The cold was becoming extreme, with an icy wind. On the march down we put the knapsacks in the boats, and each man carried two blankets. We have enough meat, but the men by this time had become very tired of biscuit. By great good luck we came on a large store of excellent flour at one village on the way down, but there was nothing in which our bakers could mix the dough, until I found a brand-new Chinese coffin in a carpenter's shop. The bakers were up all night, and next morning the Regiment had enough bread to last them to Tientsin. The tired bakers I put in the boats with the knapsacks.[2]

On arrival at Tientsin the troops were embarked on gunboats to take them down to the mouth of the Pei-ho, where they were transferred to transports for onward conveyance to Hong Kong. The 2nd Queen's sailed from Taku on 12 November, reaching Hong Kong three weeks later; from Hong Kong they had what was then considered to be a fast passage of five months back to Portsmouth. Brownlow's Punjabis left Tientsin on 13 November, transferred to transports at the mouth of the Pei-ho on the 14th, and sailed for Hong Kong on the 17th, eventually returning to Calcutta on 1 February 1861.

The King's Dragoon Guards embarked their dismounted men at Tientsin on 21 November in the steamer *Atlanta*, and lost Private Offendale, who fell overboard and drowned during the embarkation. Probyn's Horse left Tientsin on 22 November and marched to the Taku forts over roads deep in snow, covering thirty-five miles in atrocious conditions in eight hours; they were followed by the King's Dragoon Guards on the same day, who also reached Taku that evening. The

KDG embarked on 23 November; 'G' Troop reached Madras on 14 January, 'B' Troop on the 16th, 'A' Troop on the 18th, and 'F' Troop on the 24th. All four troops went on to Bangalore, arriving there between 24 January and 3 February 1861. Probyn's embarked on 26 November, spent ten days at Hong Kong en route to Calcutta and arrived back in India on 24 January 1861, whence the regiment proceeded to Sialkot.[12, 13]

A garrison had to be left at Tientsin and to garrison the Taku forts, and this comprised the 31st Regiment (East Surrey), the 60th Rifles and the 67th Regiment (Hampshires) as the infantry component, with Fane's Horse providing the cavalry, together with two and a half batteries of the Royal Artillery, a company of the Royal Engineers and a battalion of the Military Train, as well as various medical and Commissariat staff. This force was commanded by Brigadier-General Staveley.

The winter of 1860–61 was bitterly cold, and Lieutenant Hill-James, the Adjutant of the 31st Regiment (East Surrey), noted on New Year's Day:

I saw the porter issued by the Commissariat to the Regiment carried to the men's quarters by fatigue parties in sacks! It was solid ice, and had to be broken up with crowbars and picks, and then melted in pots and cauldrons before it could be measured out to the several messes, a warm and frothy beverage. The men, for the nonce, rather liked the novelty. The bread was sometimes frozen so hard it had to be sawn, instead of cut into slices.[14]

During the winter the men remained fairly healthy, but in the summer months the lack of drainage at Tientsin caused the caused the sick rate to rise, with the 67th having up to 150 men in hospital at one time. The 31st did not embark for Britain until the summer of 1863, and some of the 67th Regiment (Hampshires) remained in garrison at the Taku forts until January 1864.[3]

SOURCES
1 Royal Archives, Windsor Castle, RA VIC ADD MSS E/1, 2851.

2 Bruch Tulloch, Major-General Sir Alexander, *Recollections of Forty Years' Service*, Blackwood, 1903.

3 Atkinson, C. T., Regimental History of the Royal Hampshire Regiment, vol.1, University Press, Glasgow, 1950.

4 *Historical Records of the 20th Infantry (Duke of Cambridge's Own), Brownlow's Punjabis*, Swiss & Co, 1909.

5 Swinhoe, R., *Narrative of the North China Campaign*, Smith Elder, 1861.

6 Royal Archives, Windsor Castle, RA VIC ADD MSS E/1, 2858.

7 Wolseley, Lieut-Colonel G. J., *Narrative of the War with China in 1860*, Longman, Green, Longman & Roberts, 1862.

8 Bowlby, C. C., *An Account of the Last Mission and Death of Thomas William Bowlby*, private circulation, 1906.

9 Royal Archives, Windsor Castle, RA VIC ADD MSS E/1, 2871.

10 Porter, Major-General W., *The History of the Corps of Royal Engineers*, vol.1, 1889.

11 Royal Archives, Windsor Castle, RA VIC ADD MSS E/1, Q15.

12 Records of the King's Dragoon Guards, Regimental History of 1st The Queen's Dragoon Guards, Cardiff Castle.

13 Boyle, Major A. C., History of Probyn's Horse, Gale & Polden, 1929.

14 Langley, M., The East Surrey Regiment, Leo Cooper, 1972.

15

At the end of November Grant, having seen all his force embark, left for Hong Kong, stopping at Shanghai en route. On 5 December he wrote to the Duke of Cambridge from Shanghai:

I have to report my arrival yesterday at this place, and to state that all the troops under orders for England and India embarked and sailed from the Gulf of Pechilli before my departure from Tientsin. They were scarcely on board when the Pei-ho in several places became completely closed up with ice, and my gun boats were frozen in. These have since, I believe, cut their way through. The troops at Tientsin are very well put up, and every arrangement made for their comfort in the shape of warm clothing and furs.

I fear the drafts and depots of the Regiments at Tientsin will not be able to join their Corps before the river closes completely, also it may be very difficult to land the men at Taku. I have arranged with Admiral Hope to land them if possible, if not, to send them back to Hong Kong till next spring. Should it be the wish of Government to continue the troops at Tientsin beyond that season, I think the 60th Rifles might be ordered home. When the drafts and depots from the 31st and 67th join, they will each be upwards of 1,000 strong, which with the French force of 2,000 men will be ample for the protection of the place. One of the Native Infantry Regiments at Shanghai might also, I think, be sent back to India.[1]

In fact the 60th Rifles did not manage to return to England until the spring of 1862.

Grant continued:

The horses left at Tientsin amount to 690, inclusive of 260 mules with the Military Train, and 25 with Fane's Horse. About 800 have returned to India with the Artillery, the King's Dragoon Guards and Probyn's Horse, and about 1,400 more sold by public auction at Tientsin, which by the report of a Committee were not worth the expense of sending back. They averaged about 6 Dollars each but as soon as I receive the return, I shall forward it.

Colonel Mackenzie, Deputy Quarter Master General has been sent to Hong Kong to supervise the departure of the troops from there, as all vessels will have to land there. I regret having made a mistake in my last private letter in stating that Sir John Michel was to have command of 'The Troops in China'. I ought to have said of 'The Troops in the North of China'. The whole of the Indemnity, which by the Treaty is to be received at Tientsin, has been paid – viz 500,000 taels.[1]

It had been a quick and extremely successful campaign, bringing much credit to Grant himself, to the troops and to the staff arrangements, but Grant was not satisfied in one respect. He reported to the Duke of Cambridge:

I have had great complaints with regard to the Military Train. I had hoped to have sent a report on the subject, but unfortunately the box, which contained it, together with several other papers was stolen in the dark on embarking at the Gulf of Pechilli. It appears to me that the Officers and some of the Commanding Officers, who have been appointed to serve in the Corps, do not understand the requirements of horses; little or no attention being paid to sore backs; and no trouble taken in clothing the animals; harness not fitted or put on properly; horses not cleaned; and no effort made in securing them in the stable, or even procuring sufficient rope for the purpose. It appears to me that it would be advisable to appoint the Officers and NCO's from Cavalry and Artillery Corps, from their possessing some practical knowledge of what is required of them, and I think it would be more advantageous if the Officers were not such a high class of gentleman, and were made to understand the drudgery of the work so much required in the Military Train. I found the Officers and men looked upon themselves as a Cavalry Corps, and were not a little disappointed when they were made to do the work for which they were appointed.

As soon as I can get copies of the report, I shall forward them.[1]

He was, however, happier with the services of the Commissariat:

I am happy, however, to say there has not been the slightest difficulty in carrying on the duties of the two Armies by the Commissariat of Her Majesty's Army, and everything has gone on most satisfactorily under Mr Turner, who is an excellent Officer.[2]

Fortescue summed up the difficulties:

This, but for the interference of the diplomatic agents, was a well managed little expedition, the chief lesson of which, for the British, was that transport and supply could not be conducted under two different heads. There was constant friction between the Commissariat, which was responsible for supply, and the Navy and Military Train, which were responsible for transport afloat and ashore, but declined to take the orders or respect the wishes of the Commissariat.[3]

Sidney Herbert was able to write to Queen Victoria on 28 December:

Mr Herbert has been engaged with H.R.H. the Commander in Chief in going through the list of recommendations, and hopes shortly to have the honour of submitting a list to Your Majesty. Mr Herbert has written to Lord Palmerston with regard to the issue of a China Medal. And has also ventured to suggest to H.R.H. the Commander in Chief that the Regiments engaged should, if approved by Your Majesty, have the word 'Pekin' inscribed on their colours, on which H.R.H. will take Your Majesty's pleasure.

The China Medal was issued to all who took part, with two bars, 'Taku Forts' and 'Pekin', and the regiments involved were allowed to have inscribed upon their colours both engagements as battle honours.

Lord Elgin was made Viceroy of India, General de Montauban was raised to the French title of Count Palikao [sic], and Grant received the GCB, together with a letter from Sidney Herbert:

The public here are, I think, very pleased with the way everything has been done in China, firmness, skill, success, a first-rate General, a capital Staff, an excellent Commissariat, and a good Medical Department are four things the English public are especially pleased to see, and the more so when all are got together.[4]

Fortescue wrote of Grant:

He had a fine force of hardened, seasoned men, and he so contrived matters that there should be little sickness and no discontent, or, in other words, that there should be no avoidable privation, hardship and fatigue. Knowing that their General would never call upon them for any unusual effort without good cause, the men always responded readily and heartily to any such summons and, in fact, would do anything for him. No man ever more thoroughly understood the British soldier, and, for all that he had read no books, not many men have better understood war than this gentle, kindly, pious, daring lancer, who could play as skilfully on the hearts of his men as on the strings of his beloved violoncello.[3]

Honours were generously bestowed upon other leading figures in the campaign; Brigadier Pattle and Lieutenant-Colonel Sayer of the King's Dragoon Guards, Colonel Spence of the 31st Regiment (East Surrey), Lieutenant-Colonel Mann and Major Fisher of the Royal Engineers were all among those who were awarded the CB. Captain Fane of Fane's Horse, Captain Brownlow of Brownlow's Punjabis, and Captain Miller of the 67th Regiment (Hampshires) received brevet majorities. The 44th Regiment (Essex) had won two Victoria Crosses, and the 67th Regiment had been awarded four; all six had been gained at the storming of the Taku forts.

Perhaps the last word remains with Bruce Tulloch of the Royal Scots: 'The Canton Coolie Corps were very plucky, even holding the scaling ladders for our men storming the large Taku fort. The Tartars, who were also a fine fighting lot, would have made good cavalrymen.'[5]

SOURCES
1 Royal Archives, Windsor Castle, RA VIC ADD MSS E/1, 2928.
2 Royal Archives, Windsor Castle, RA VIC ADD MSS E/1, 2858.
3 Fortescue, Hon. J. W., *History of the Army*, vol.13, Macmillan, 1917, ch.55.
4 Royal Archives, Windsor Castle, RA VIC ADD MSS E/1, Q15.
5 Bruce Tulloch, Major-General Sir Alexander, *Recollections of Forty Years' Service*, Blackwood, 1903.

APPENDIX A

Total Effective Strengths

January, 1860: at Hong Kong and Canton	5,757
March, 1860: at Hong Kong and Canton	6,128
April, 1860: at Hong Kong, Canton, Kowloon and Chusan	7,456
May, 1860	16,909
July, 1860	15,901
August, 1860	15,970
September, 1860	16,596
October, 1860	16,517
November, 1860	16,418
December, 1860: North China	5,450
Canton	5,160
en route to former stations	10,970

APPENDIX B

Regimental Strengths, August 1860

Brigadier Pattle, KDG
Lt-Col Walker, Queen's Bays, AQMG

	Officers	Other Ranks	Horses
King's Dragoon Guards	17	314	284
Probyn's Horse	18	454	441
Fane's Horse	14	330	296

1ST INFANTRY DIVISION
Major-General Sir John Michel

1st Brigade

Brigadier Staveley, 31st Foot

1st Royal Scots	34	697
31st Regiment (East Surrey)	31	1,097
Loodhiana Sikhs (at Shanghai)	12	664

2nd Brigade

Brigadier Sutton

2nd Regiment (Queen's)	32	762
60th Rifles	31	873
15th Punjabis	15	943

2ND INFANTRY DIVISION
Major-General Sir Robert Napier

3rd Brigade

Brigadier Reeves

3rd Regiment (The Buffs)	33	1,181
44th Regiment (Essex)	31	1,097
8th Punjabis	14	785

4th Brigade

67th Regiment (Hampshire)	34	1,013

99th Regiment (Wiltshire)	31	1,010
19th Punjabis	15	943
Royal Marine Light Infantry	36	903
Royal Artillery	55	1,869
Royal Engineers	14	282
Military Train	15	267
Commissariat		24
Army Hospital Corps		137

APPENDIX C

Officers of the King's Dragoon Guards Serving in China, 1860

Lt-Col Thomas Pattle, Commanding Cavalry Brigade
Lt-Col Robert Sayer, Officer Commanding
Major Herbert Slade, in command Details
Captain Emmanuel Bradbury, in command 'B' Troop
Captain Henry Alexander, in command 'F' Troop
Captain Walker Wingfield, in command 'A' Troop
Captain James Gunter, in command 'G' Troop
Lt Henry Sidney, Details
Lt Alfred Greaves, 'A' Troop
Lt Charles Hubback, Details
Lt Harper Crewe, 'B' Troop
Lt William Marsland, 'G' Troop
Cornet Frederick Sedley, 'B' Troop
Assistant Surgeon Edward McSheehy
Veterinary Surgeon Thacker

ON ATTACHMENT

Lt McLeod, from 1st Madras Light Cavalry, 'F' Troop
Cornet Say, from 1st Madras Light Cavalry, 'F' Troop
Assistant Surgeon Baynham, from the Madras Army
Assistant Surgeon Burkett, from the 74th Highlanders (HLI)

Bibliography

Allgood, Lieut G., *The China War, 1860*, Longmans Green & Co., 1901.
Anglesey, Marquess of, *History of the British Cavalry*, vol.2, 1851–1871, Leo Cooper, 1975.
Atkinson, C. T., *Regimental History of the Royal Hampshire Regiment*, vol.1, University Press Glasgow, 1950.
Belfield, E., *The Queen's Dragoon Guards*, Leo Cooper, 1978.
Blaxland, G., *The Buffs*, Leo Cooper, 1972.
Bowlby, C. C., *An Account of the Last Mission and Death of Thomas William Bowlby*, private circulation, 1906.
Boyle, Major A. C., *History of Probyn's Horse*, Gale & Polden, 1929.
Bruce Tulloch, Major-General Sir Alexander, *Reflections of Forty Years' Service*, Blackwood, 1903.
Cantlie, Lieut-General Sir Neil, *A History of the Army Medical Department*, vol.2, Churchill Livingstone, 1974.
Carter, T., *Historical Records of the 44th, or East Sussex Regiment*, W. O. Mitchell, 1864.
Dunne, J. H., *From Calcutta to Pekin*, Sampson Low & Son, 1861.
Fortescue, Hon. J. W., *History of the Army*, vol.13, Macmillan, 1917, ch.55.
Gibson, Tom, *The Wiltshire Regiment*, Leo Cooper, 1969.
Haswell, J., *The Queen's Royal Regiment*, Hamish Hamilton, 1967.
Historical Record of the 20th Infantry (Duke of Cambridge's Own), Brownlow's Punjabis, Swiss & Co., 1909.
Hudson, General Sir H., *History of the 19th King George's Own Lancers, 1858–1921*, Gale & Polden, 1937.
Hurd, Douglas, *The Arrow War*, Collins, 1967.
Inglis, Brian, *The Opium War*, Hodder & Stoughton, 1976.
Kenrick, Colonel N. C. E., *The Story of the Wiltshire Regiment*, Gale & Polden, 1963.
Knollys, H., *Incidents in the China War of 1860*, Blackwood, 1875.
Langley, Michael, *The East Surrey Regiment*, Leo Cooper, 1972.
Maxwell, Captain E. L., *History of the 11th King Edward's Own Lancers*, A. C. Curtis, 1914.
Porter, Major-General W., *The History of the Royal Engineers*, vol.1, 1889.
Records of the King's Dragoon Guards, Regimental Museum, 1st The Queen's Dragoon Guards, Cardiff.
Selby, John, *The Paper Dragon*, Arthur Barker, 1968.
Swinhoe, Robert, *Narrative of the North China Campaign of 1860*, Smith, Elder, 1861.
Wolseley, Lieut-Colonel G. J., *Narrative of the War with China in 1860*, Longman, Green, Longman & Roberts, 1862.

Wolseley, Lieut-Colonel G. J., *The Story of a Soldier's Life*, vol.2, London, 1903.

Wood, H. Fairlie, *The King's Royal Rifle Corps*, Hamish Hamilton, 1967.

Royal Archives, Windsor Castle.

Lieutenant-Colonel G. J. Wolseley, by Beato, 1860 (courtesy of the Director, National Army Museum).

ABOVE *Fane's Horse on board ship, en route from Talienwan to Pehtang:
sketch by C. Wirgman for* Illustrated London News *(BBC Hulton Picture
Library),* BELOW *Sikh sowar, by Beato, 1860 (courtesy of the Director,
National Army Museum).*

Pathan officer of Fane's Horse, by Beato, 1860 (courtesy of the Director, National Army Museum).

Men of the 15th Punjabis, by Beato, 1860 (courtesy of the Director, National Army Museum).

ABOVE *Musbee Sikhs of the 15th Punjabis, by Beato, 1860 (courtesy of the Director, National Army Museum).* BELOW *The British and French flags flying at the fort at Pehtang, by Beato, 1860 (BBC Hulton Picture Library).*

ABOVE *An officer and two troopers of the King's Dragoon Guards reconnoitring the canals between Tangku and the Taku forts. Drawing by H. Hope Crealock, 1860 (courtesy of the Director, National Army Museum).* BELOW *The entrance to the north Taku fort, by Beato, 1860. (BBC Hulton Picture Library).*

ABOVE *The entrance to the north Taku fort from the inside, by Beato, 1860 (BBC Hulton Picture Library).* BELOW *Interior of the north Taku fort after capture, by Beato, 1860 (courtesy of the Director, National Army Museum).*

ABOVE *Major Dighton Probyn VC, leading his men at Chang-kia-wan. Drawing by H. Hope Crealock, 1860 (courtesy of the Director, National Army Museum).* BELOW *Charge of the King's Dragoon Guards at Palichao. Drawing by H. Hope Crealock, 1860 (Regimental Museum of 1st The Queen's Dragoon Guards, Cardiff Castle).*

Index

120, 122, 123, 124, 130, 131,
133, 138, 139, 141, 143, 155,
156, 159
Punjabis, 8th (Brownlow's), 6,
16, 28, 33–4, 37, 46, 58, 88,
89, 97, 127, 128, 148, 149,
154, 156, 162
Punjabis, 11th, 6; 15th, 6, 9, 16,
28, 37, 44, 51, 64, 67, 106,
109, 111, 112, 123, 151, 156;
19th, 6, 17, 28, 37, 41, 100
1st Royal Scots, 7, 14, 16, 28, 33,
36, 41–2, 44, 50, 51–2, 61, 65,
67, 68–9, 70–1, 96, 97, 99,
127, 148–9, 156
2nd Regiment (Queen's), 6, 9, 16,
21, 28, 44, 48, 49, 51, 67, 107,
109, 111, 118, 121, 123, 139–
40, 156
3rd Regiment (The Buffs), 6, 9,
16, 28, 37, 46, 58, 59, 73, 74,
88–9, 96
31st Regiment (East Surrey), 6, 9,
14, 15, 16, 28, 44, 61, 156,
157, 159, 162
44th Regiment (Essex), 6, 9, 10,
14, 16, 28, 33, 46, 53, 58,
60–1, 73, 74, 83, 84, 85, 86,
91, 96, 162
60th Rifles, 6, 9, 16, 28, 39–40,
44, 49, 50, 51, 64, 67, 68, 69,
70, 96, 101, 107, 127, 128,
131, 150–1, 154, 155, 157, 159
67th Regiment (Hampshire), 6, 9,
16, 17, 23, 24, 25, 28, 34, 41,
46, 53, 58, 59, 80, 81, 82–3,
84, 85, 86, 127, 149, 154, 157,
159, 162
87th Regiment (Irish Fusiliers), 6,
14, 15, 16
99th Regiment (Wiltshire), 6, 9,
14, 17, 23, 24, 25, 28, 34, 36,
41, 56, 87, 97, 101, 103, 105,
109, 111, 112, 113, 122, 127,
129, 140, 154
Royal Artillery, 6, 7, 15, 16, 18,
20, 23, 24, 26, 27, 28, 40, 41,
44, 46, 50, 52, 57, 58, 59, 60,
61, 67, 68, 70, 76, 80, 81, 82,

83, 85, 86–7, 88, 96, 97, 99,
100, 101, 103, 104, 105–6,
107, 109, 111, 112, 120, 122,
127, 128, 130–1, 132, 141,
148, 149, 154, 155, 156, 157,
159
Royal Engineers, 6, 15, 16, 23,
28, 45, 47, 54, 58, 65, 67, 80,
83, 84, 85, 91, 109, 149, 157,
162
Royal Marines, 2, 23, 30, 38, 47,
58, 83, 84, 87, 91, 94, 101,
103, 109, 122, 128, 155
Rennie, Surgeon, 36, 37
Rigaud, Maj, 60th Rifles, 67
Rogers, Lieut, VC, Essex, 85–6, 91
Rotton, Maj, RA, 23, 44, 58, 59, 99
Royal Scots, see 1st Royal Scots
under Regiments
Ross, Col, Royal Scots, 7
Royal Artillery, see Regiments
Royal Engineers, see Regiments
Royal Marines, see Regiments
Royal Navy, 2, 3, 26–7, 38, 42, 47,
52, 80–1, 82, 83, 93, 105–6, 161
Russell, Lord John, 3, 5, 25

Sankolinsin, Gen, 2, 65, 73, 88, 94,
110, 117, 122, 131, 132, 141,
142, 143
Sargent, Lieut-Col, Buffs, 58
Sayer, Lieut-Col, KDG, 9, 10, 162
Shanghai, 1, 3, 12, 20, 22, 23, 27,
29, 30, 31, 36, 88, 96, 153, 159
Shantung, 30, 31, 35
SHIPS:
    Adventure, 47; *Alfred*,
    44; *Arracan*, 45; *Assistance*, 27;
    Athlete, 46, 47; *Atlanta*, 156;
    Australian, 44, 47; *Bentinck*, 44;
    Bosphorus, 44, 47; *Brandon*, 46;
    British Flag, 46; *Burlington*, 44;
    Bustard, 96; *Calcutta*, 29; *Cambodia*, 46; *Cambrian*, HMS, 42;
    Chesapeake, HMS, 68; *City of
    Poonah*, 46; *Clarendon*, 46;
    Clown, HMS, 80, *Coromandel*,
    HMS, 94; *Cressy*, 46, 47;
    Dalhousie, 46; *Daniel Rankin*,

MISERABLE LOVE POETRY AND
OTHER POEMS

Miserable Love Poetry and Other Poems

ANTHONY WHITE

Beastling Publishing

CONTENTS

~ ~

Why must it have been

~ ~

Commonplace Episode

~ ~

Love, don't be sad

~ ~

I have written enough about love

~ ~

For Yvonne

~ ~

Consolations

II

Other Poems

~ ~

Faust

~ ~

To Yvonne

First Printed by Beastling Publishing, 2021

ANTHONY WHITE
Miserable Love Poetry
and
Other Poems

I

Miserable Love Poetry

I bent down on my knees and said
If you can love me now you stand so tall
I'll give you everything. She touched my head
And somewhere far above me said
Is that all?

REMEMBER WHEN WE SAID

Remember when we said

We must meet

To remember that time

When we sat

And remembered how we met

And everything that led

From that

Remember how you said

Yes - but no!

I've just remembered

I'm busy all that week

And then we go

To China; but we'll speak

Again in September

Remember how I said

That's okay

But you will remember, won't you

And then I heard

Nothing for an age

Not a word

Until *I* phoned *you*

And reminded you, you'd promised to remember

And you hadn't remembered

And you must have known how much I'd be upset

And you said - *No, I forget*

THE JUDGEMENT OF PARIS

I am Athena and I have riches and power

Choose me and I will give you as my dower

Empires.

I am Aretha and I am skilful and wise

Choose me and we will live above the skies

And not expire.

My name's Apple - what you see is what you get

Choose me quick - these attributes won't last, though they beget

Desire.

He chose Desire

I HEARD A MAN ON THE RADIO SAY

I heard a man on the radio say -

Talking of the music he had listened to in his youth -

That when you are a teenager you choose -

Even though you are too young to have known such a thing -

To play those songs that tell of broken love affairs -

As if – no, not as if, but truly -

Lost love seems more real than anything you know -

As if those songs about love that's over

Speak to you even though it's before

You've ever had love, before you've ever been in love -

And, having said all that, he played

An old, familiar song,

One of those songs

In which 'brown eyes' rhymes with 'goodbyes',

'Lovin' heart' with 'torn apart',

'By my side' with 'tears I've cried'.

It only took three minutes to say all that.

On the clifftop

Through a gap between the poplars and the pines,

Beyond the miles of zinc-grey sea,

The horizon glitters -

A thin line of light you could never reach

No matter how young and fast you are.

It is always just as far away,

And it won't come in with the tide.

In the high street

A man bent over a guitar sings, roughly, a song.

It takes you a while to recognise

Bobby Shafto's Gone to Sea,

He is playing it as if it's a tragedy.

You drop a coin inside his hat

Say *Thanks for the memory.*

Back home you turn the radio on.

This time you hear a woman's voice

Telling you about mindfulness

How it can help you to cope with painful thoughts.

You listen for a minute, switch it off,

Saying sorry but now I'm fully grown

There's nothing you can do for my heart of stone.

You wait for the repeat, of the man

Talking about lost love and about those songs

That made melancholy sound more appealing

Than happiness or joy

When you were still a boy.

SESTINA

I will write you a fucking sestina and you still won't care.

I shall stare at the laptop waiting for your answer.

After a week you will send me a one-line e-mail:

I like it! a smiley face and a single kiss

Is all I will get for my outpouring of love.

Do you wonder that I am bitter and your slave?

You cannot – or can you? - have wanted me for your slave.

Even if you knew what I felt, and didn't care,

You must have known that all I write about love

Is addressed to you, and's for you to answer,

Yet all I receive is a hug and a chaste kiss,

A tardy, unwilling reply to my passionate e-mail.

I wish I could write you a letter instead of an e-mail.

The list of emojis doesn't have one for 'slave',

And there's no weight of meaning in typing an 'x' for a kiss.

Between the lines I can tell you how much I care,

But not enough for you to have to answer

In words that have anything at all to do with love.

And that's that. I have had enough of writing about love -

Writing to myself (even though I send *you* the e-mail).

I have no question waiting for an answer,

All I have's this sestina over which I slave,

And I wonder sometimes if it is this I care

For more than getting from you a tender kiss.

But my heart aches still when I dream about that kiss,

And of you, and of begging you for your love,

And I wonder if I have taken too much care

Not to hurt you with what I write in the e-mail -

Romantic love, like this tricky form, can make a slave

Of anyone who can't find an easy answer.

Oh love! Oh Love! tell me tell me the answer.

Is it that simple - to want no more than a kiss?

Would that free me to be your equal, no longer your slave?

Would I know at last what it means to love,

To please you, to be kind, forget the bloody e-mail,

To forget the pangs of passion and truly care?

Answer me, dear, and I beg you, in words of love.

Kiss your poor slave who writes to you this e-mail.

I press 'send' and place this poor verse in your care.

WHAT HURTS MOST

Writing down the memories that hurt

I try to be complete.

I write them out in measurements of feet -

My home, my school, my friends, my work.

You will notice what is missing from the above.

I try to be complete,

But it hurts too much, from my head to my feet,

To write of love, of love, of love.

THE SWEATER

How is it human beings haven't changed?

Still can't tell right from wrong,

All the way from the Stone Age

To drone-dropped bombs.

She lent me – this is a long time ago – a sweater.

She gave it to me because I was feeling cold.

She told me I could keep it - this was later.

It was navy-blue and crew necked.

I can say, now I'm a poet,

That it smelled of hope and of regret

But it didn't - it smelled of her sweet scent.

I treated it with care and with respect

Pressed it to my face and to my breast

Trying to preserve the perfumed present

Which was her.

I'm sorry that you feel that way

Is a line that ends with a full stop.

I begged her to continue- *"and?"*-

Even though I knew that adding to it

Sounds as though you are taking something away.

The sweater lost her scent after a bit.

Should I wear it? I wondered; or write about it?

YEARNING FOR LOVE

These days we begin our infrequent meetings

With smiles and touches, near-ecstatic greetings,

As though it's showtime after far too few rehearsals.

We exchange banalities, step apart

To say *Let me look at you - what's the art*

You have of staying young and beautiful?

We tell each other that we *didn't* prefer

This café when it was cheap and cheerful -

Its smell of bacon frying, sound of Radio One.

We like, we say, the way they've done it up,

Play punk music as background noise.

And, as we sit and stir our café noirs

We just about make out Patti Smith snarling

We don't need your fucking shit

And we laugh, as if it's funny, for a bit.

We used, I'm certain, to be adamant

That prose was a hardly-spoken-of, distant

Relative of poetry, the real thing.

Our lives, we meant, were poems, all moments

Heightened, all nights red, red roses.

No-one would ever say my life's like *prose.*

These days we choose our words more carefully.

"I like your coat", I say; "it suits you".

Its lapels, its pockets, its buttons, the way it

Holds your scarf to your neck, the way it

Comes down to your knees. Once a coat

Was a thing to get quickly out of,

Its warmth and colour of no interest to me.

We've been through what we've seen and what we've read

How you finally cleared your credit card debt

How the lump in your armpit was benign.

We agree how sweet it is that all is well.

I notice they have games - we could play Scrabble?

When you think that once...Oh, aren't we terrible?

We say goodbye like mourners on Good Friday.

I get all the warmth of your coat. Don't be a stranger.

We must do this more often. No. Really.

WHAT WAS SHE THEN

What was She *then* -

When I was young

And spending my heart's youth -

That now is lost

To half-blind eyes

That squint at books for truth?

Was She – the gold

And lustrous hair,

The sparkling eyes

Aglow with tears

That now are dull and dry?

Or was She – the soul

I could not see,

That gave such joy, such pain?

And where's that now

And how transformed?

Is it, too, aged and stained?

No answer comes -

Not yesterday,

Today, or other days.

There is no map

That marks the place

The thread snapped in the maze.

IN THOSE DAYS WE WROTE LETTERS

In those days we wrote letters.

One night I wrote

I'm in love with you

And signed my name

And sealed it, then

Wondered whether to send it.

These days we have email, text,

Which are quick and sort of free

So better.

Neither do we have to observe the niceties

Of beginning *Dear You*

And writing *Love Me* to end it.

IT'S AN OLD IDEA, AT LEAST
TO ME

It's an old idea, at least to me,

That Love will return, but empty-handed,

No matter how you beg Her *Leave me be*

In dreams that slip your understanding.

Ah spare me! Venus; let me be.

Once again you set me on my shanks.

There have been so many meetings, partings

At so many bus stops, taxi-ranks,

So many passions that turned into farces,

So many walks back home on canal banks.

Yes, love will return but empty-handed.

The tormentor will wind the rack.

Believing you have answers he is minded

To keep on winding 'til you crack -

All he asks of you is to be candid.

The only remedy for love is song,

But art is too brief, life too long.

We go on singing all the time there's light

And now 'tis night. And now, he said, 'tis night.

POEM TO YOU

I address this poem to You

As if you will ever see it

I talk to You in this poem

As if you will ever hear it

I write to an anonymous You

Certain you'll never read it

The chances are I shall bury it in my blog

Read it to seven people in a bar

The chances really are a million to one

That you'll come across it by chance

Yet I address it to You

And even if that million-to-one shot comes in

How could you possibly know that I mean You?

(I know other women, you know.)

But all the same I am saying this to You

Whatever do I mean by doing so?

LOVE SONG

If only you were different

And I were different

And we lived in another place

In another time

We might be lovers

If only you were dead

And I were dead

We might be remembered

Like Romeo and Juliet

As great lovers

Live for the moment! you advised me once.

Yes, life is for living, for sure.

If only we'd known

What moments are for

We might have been lovers

If only you loved me

And I you

And you told me

And I told you

We might become lovers

DO YOU SEE WHAT I SEE?

Do you see what I see? said the poet to one most fond,

That cloud shaped like a camel in the sky?

His love replied: I don't; it's just a cloud in the beyond,

A veil of white against the blue so high.

Alas, the poet cried; I feel our hearts can never rhyme.

You do not see the world the way I do.

His lover smiled: We've more than eyes to see ourselves in time.

See the beauty of the white against the blue.

The poet looked; the cloud had changed, was shaped more like a whale,

He said: I cannot trust myself to speak.

His love replied: Be silent then, and do not think you fail,

But press your cheek against my blushing cheek.

The poet touched, and felt the life in the face pressed against his.

He closed his eyes against the blinding light.

His lover mussed his hair and whispered: This is all there is -

Unmoving blue and changing shapes of white.

WHY MUST IT HAVE BEEN

Why must it have been

A chance irrevocably lost?

Like an episode in a novel

You realise, chapters later,

Was the key to the young man's character,

The outline of his destiny,

The rest of the book just a colouring-in.

Why could it not have been

A comic incident, slapstick almost,

Cleaned up with the next day's hangover?

Ah, youth! What serious fools we were

Inking our skins with tattoos

As if to say: *I'll never be old;*

I shall always be like this.

And you are.

COMMONPLACE EPISODE

You asked me back for coffee and I came.

You put some music on at such low volume

I could hardly hear it, but the background hum

Was pleasant, as was the indoors of your home.

You boiled the water and told me about your dream.

I made myself pretty snug in your living-room.

We liked each other well enough that night.

When morning came, we woke up to the sight

Of ashtrays, stains of wine and Coffeemate.

You busied yourself with putting things back to rights -

Your mum was coming at ten to take you out.

I had to go and couldn't find my coat.

Yes, I think that's more or less how it went.

I wish I could remember your dream, but I can't.

For a while I lived inside your exquisite scent.

We loved all the places and the time we spent

(Though dawn over Zagreb was a non-event).

We came back with a taste for Crème de Menthe.

I knew it was over before you finished it

Nonetheless, it was hard not to feel hurt -

Your home was warmer than mine, I liked your cat,

How we'd moved from Iggy Pop to Arvo Pärt.

I'm not sure I still loved you after that

But I got over it, bit by bit.

LOVE, DON'T BE SAD

Love, don't be sad, for time will pass, and pains

That now seem permanent will heal.

As, underneath the crushing of Time's wheel,

New grass will grow when come the summer rains,

So broke hearts will pump, blood flow to the scars,

Pale faces blush again, Love herself blush

To find how little strength she has to crush,

Or build around your heart her prison bars,

What once you seemed to care for, now seem nought -

That face, embrace, that voice, all traces fade.

Love, Love will pass, and Time unmake the made.

Careless of care, love, you will Time report

That all is healed, recovered, love's pain passed.

Don't worry, love; this time will be the last.

I HAVE WRITTEN ENOUGH
ABOUT LOVE

I have written enough about love

And said nothing at all.

The dancing, the drinking, the weddings

Meant nothing at all.

There were moments, of course, there were

Moments when life was a ball,

But I've written enough about love

To know that was all.

And now, wrapped up warm, wearing gloves

In the old peoples' hall,

We chuckle at youngsters today -

How they rise! How they fall!

We shrink in the past, and the present

Means nothing at all.

But the past is no good; it's the place

Where the old voices call

You have written too much about love

And said nothing at all.

FOR YVONNE

I never never never never never

Want to meet anybody ever again – ever

I mean it I really really really really do

I never again want to hear anyone say

It's me - it isn't you

OR *I need my space*

OR *I think we should take some time out*

(A trial separation is the idea

But the key word is separation...)

This is the living grid of shiftlessness

That passes for maturity, even sophisticatedness

We were not, after all, meant for each other

But I still love you like a friend or brother

Stuff that - what happened to romantic love?

Why is it dead and gone

Living on only in song?

Yours is the most meaningful, deepest...

Friendship... I've had in years

Don't trash it because you can't have everything

I'm really fond of you; I love you dearly

But we're not teenagers any more

And you're acting like a child

Don't you know how selfish you are being

I'm a decent man and mild

And, may I say, you always

Will be a priority

Not exclusive though

You can't have everything your way

Besides, I'm not looking for a relationship right now

And anyway you're too good for me

You'll always be special

I ask Yvonne Do they ever say

I need to get my head sorted out

or better still

I need to get my karma sorted out

I bet they do

Maybe we're just not meant to be

No-one's to blame

I'm not good enough for you

Yes, any old excuse will do

For leaving you.

CONSOLATIONS

Hayley Mills Helen Mirren Gina Lollobrigida

Sophie Marceau Ava Gardner Debbie Harry Cher

Rita Hayworth Christine Keeler Cyndi Lauper Doris Day

Lulu Claudia Cardinale Twiggy Ludivine Sagnier

Mandy Rice-Davies Romy Schneider Isabella Rossellini

Ingrid Bergman Virna Lisi Diana Rigg Natasha Kinski

Louise Brooks Christina Hendricks Monica Bellucci

Audrey Hepburn Susan Sarandon Mae West Vivian Leigh

Scarlet Johannson Lesley Caron Marilyn Monroe Sandie Shaw

Brigitte Bardot Raquel Welch Kim Novak Hedy Lamarr

Natalie Wood Marianne Faithfull Sophia Loren Heather Graham

Joanna Lumley Elizabeth Taylor Diana Dors Honor Blackman

Jacqueline Bissett Jane Birkin Joni Mitchell Grace Jones

Petula Clark Kirsty McColl Jean Shrimpton Clara Bow

Carole Lombard Kathy Kirby

Diana Quick Isabelle Adjani

Jenny Agutter Jayne Mansfield

Grace Kelly Tuesday Weld

I could go on, but time is short,

(And on, and on, and on).

II

Other Poems

FAUST

Faust said to the devil I'll sell you my soul for a dollar

The devil replied, If you want anything just hollar

You can have power, riches, women, all kinds of stuff

Anything, as long as I get your soul when you snuff.

Faust said, No, a dollar will do; it's more than enough

EVERYONE IS ASLEEP BUT HER

Everyone is asleep but her

Every night she waits for something to perfect it

The embers of a fire

The sound of rain

Something that would make a perfect end

And let her close her eyes

Depart in peace the hectic, humdrum day

She knows they think her slightly mad

Waiting in the dark to hear a fox's howl

The wit-woo of an owl

Everyone is asleep but her

It is her time of the day

Outside on the verandah

A shawl about her shoulders

She curls into that slight insanity

And huddles like a witch to conjure the sounds -

She hears the moon complain,

The sighing of the trees, the flowers' echo,

The echoes that were muffled in the day

She knows they think her slightly mad

They are indoors and sleeping

They have turned the lights off in the billiard room

Left their brandy glasses empty

All through the day she has longed for this moment of night

Once the embers have died

And the rain has stopped

She shakes herself and stands

In the moonlit dark

Sparks fly from her shawl into the night

DOES YOUR RESTLESS HEART
MEAN I'M STILL ON YOUR
MIND

Is this a line from a Neil Young song

Or is it one of mine?

I woke up this morning, a book in my hands

Forgot what I'd read; it happens that way.

There's this private dick with a snap-brim hat

Glass of rye on his desk and

A smoke in the side of his mouth

Who, for so many bucks a day, plus expenses,

Gets coshed and drugged and shot at

While a snake-hipped blonde blows smoke rings in his ear.

He pulls her to him, kisses her, knowing she's no good.

He solves the crime, most people die.

He's bitterer than ever after that; drinks more rye.

There now. I don't need to read that book.

What can it tell me that I don't know already?

I woke up this morning; found a blonde in my bed.

This one was brunette, and she was dead.

They always are.

Before I called the cops, I fixed some breakfast.

She said Hey That's No Way To Fry An Egg

And I thought

Is that a verse from a Leonard Cohen song

Or is it one of hers?

Knock it off, sweetheart, I snarled,

You're in too deep. You think that Joey Money

Doesn't know, this minute, where you are?

His tough guy, Muscles Maddocks, is right outside.

What if I invite him in for coffee?

What then?

Yeah, that's how it was when I fell asleep,

I remember now.

The cops were soothing in my ear:

Just tell the truth for once.

We'll make it easy for you, gumshoe;

She pulled a hatpin on you,

You shot her dead in self-defence.

Give up the dumbshow.

I needed to think...

Does your restless heart mean I'm still on your mind?

Try Lucky's cardiac vinegar; proved to do this,

Guaranteed to do that.

You'll never feel that restless heart again.

After the commercial break they let me go.

The one guy hated to do it

But his partner said *It's okay,*

We know where to find him.

Outside, the blonde was in the Packard with the big white wheels.

Get in, she snapped, and put her foot down.

We drank Tom Collins in the bar of the Brooks Hotel,

The place they use in all the PI movies.

What did you tell them?

She breathed the question through her scarlet lips

And a cloud of cigarette smoke.

Listen sweetheart, I'm tired, I said.

I woke up this morning with a corpse in my bed

And the cops have me in the frame,

And now you ask me -

Please mister, she began -

Oh, it's mister now, is it?

It wasn't mister last night, was it?

It was O Johnny, yes Johnny.

Well, I can't remember if I paid the rent this morning,

And it's the day for paying the rent

And I don't want to lose my home; I like it -

It's good for sleeping in, and drinking coffee in

And -

Oh, go to hell.

And then I kissed her.

And then I kissed her -

No, that's not one of mine, is it?

IF ONLY

If only if only if only

The things your mam told you were true

That if you say your prayers

You will climb heaven's stairs

On the day the grim reaper reaps you

If only if only if only

Time had stood still when you were still young

And though aged ninety-three

You'd be fit as a flea

Still running around having fun

If only if only if only

Your lovers were just as you'd dreamed

As good in your bed

As they were in your head

Love as wonderful as it had seemed

If only if only if only

Success and fortune were your fate

That through all of your days

You received the world's praise

Good things handed to you on a plate

Much more likely is that you are skint

Have no lovers or friends, and are lonely

And when the time goes

And you turn up your toes

They will carve on your gravestone *'If only'*

DROWNING MY SORROWS

We had started the night at Dunlevy's Bar and Lounge

The place where Mildred sat from five to seven

With the evening crossword by her glass of stout

Woe betide the man who offered to help her

And then we were at Mulhern's with the man himself

Where John Doyle in his mackintosh and hat

Had the corner stool and never budged

You'd have thought his arse was glued on to that seat

And then O'Brien's (aka the Kozy Kip Bar)

Where medical students would try the yard of ale;

James Lawless's, where Pat, who never washed,

So sweetly sang the songs of Donegal

At last, at Brady's, you told me all your sorrows

I was too drunk by then to take it in

But they sounded very like my own sorrows

I didn't cry, I took it on the chin

Hard not to - it's the chin I've had for years

Down which the Guinness soaks into my beard.

THE LAST OF SUMMER

...such beautiful days

I saw sheep in fields

Trees on high ridges against the sky

Horses in a field with sheep

I saw water rippling under low bridges

Churches of flint down dead-end lanes

Old cottages with tiny windowpanes

Long-horned cows that stopped chewing until I had passed.

Chickens!

And yet I need my medicines and drugs

And long sleeps and dreams

Of things that never happened

And will never happen now

If only I could stay here with the horses

The horses and the healing sheep.

LASCIA LA SPINA

Of all the places that hurt -

The joints of her hands, her backbone, her hips and wrists -

The place that hurts most is her heart.

Her heart is the size of her arthritic fist.

She knows the declension so well -

"I will always love you" to "We'll always be friends" -

As though she was taught at school

How the story begins and ends.

The pleasure it used to give her is no more.

Memory mocks her; it's ancient history.

Her torment has at its core

Memory having no mercy.

Just catching a word starts it off.

It could be a word as harmless as 'night-time' or 'closer'.

An overheard song is enough:

Lascia la spina, cogli la rosa

"Lascia la spina, cogli la rosa; tu vai cercando il tuo dolor"

Leave the thorn, gather the rose; you go searching for your pain.

LARGE CONCRETE STRUCTURE

The cherry blossom tells us Spring has come

The cherry blossom tells us Spring has come

There are necessary hormones, rising sap

Come, sit beneath the blossom while it lasts

As pretty as a picture you were then

You were as pretty as a picture then

And because you can only think of time as passing

You took a photograph I still possess

But I remember it better than yesterday

I remember it better than I remember yesterday

You beneath the blossom at our picnic

Plump with youth and promise in the Spring

Here, there is memory and place and no anger

We knew no anger then

We had no reason

Rage came later, for no good reason

For no reason at all

But here, there is memory and place and no anger

There were ponies

We were dare-devils, climbing trees

As high as the lowest branch

And then those shiny boots, the click and clack

You heard before you saw them

Then rage had its season

The speed of change comes quickly

The blossom grows, goes quickly

One year the picture of you under the blossom

The next an abstract of something that might be blossom

Your departure not even hinted at

Your presence not even hidden

I look for you in this large concrete structure

I take for a work of art, a structure

That once had use, though no longer,

Not these days. It is labelled 'Large Concrete Structure'

And I admire it more, these days,

Than the lovely cherry blossom in the Spring

UNCLE RAY

Once he had had a few beers

You always wanted to hear

What Uncle Ray

Had to say.

He didn't change over the years

He'd sing *The Death of Nelson* out of tune

Stick a balloon

Up his Christmas jumper

Tell us that it wasn't just a bump

But a baby on the way

That was typical Uncle Ray.

Once he told us, with a laugh,

that he hadn't been able to get out of the bath that morning

Had thought he must have had a stroke,

But it wasn't, it was just some kind of warning

And he laughed, did Uncle Ray.

When I was of an age,

He told me other kinds of stories

Like the one about his mate, Len,

Who had got so drunk he'd woken up in Dumfries

From where he'd phoned his wife

Oh, my; what a glorious life.

When he died, our Auntie Em

Found him on the kitchen floor at 3am

He must have stood up to open another bottle

There was whisky all over the lino

His tongue was stuck in his open mouth

There were fifty cigarette butts in the ash tray

That was the end of Uncle Ray.

Auntie Em knelt in the whisky and gave Uncle Ray a kiss

Despite all the laughter, she had known it would end like this.

PETER AND THE HORSES

When we were on our third pint

I asked Pete to tell me the one about the horses

Oh, he said, you mean that time they got out in the night

And broke down fifteen fence posts

And got into the cemetery

And trampled all the flowers

And shat on the lawns

And then walked across the A10

(Jesus - the A10!) and came out of all that without a scratch on them?

And I got up in the morning and found them gone

And had to follow their trail of destruction

Before I found them in Jimmy Nayler's field?

And Jimmy not minding a bit

But me having to pour oil on troubled waters at the cemetery,

And taking them a box of doughnuts as a peace offering?

No, I said; not that one.

I mean the one that's not really about the horses

The one where you bought your son the horse

And paid two thousand pounds for it

And he told you soon after that he wasn't interested any more

And you were so cross you wanted to tell him

And you asked me – me, of all people – what you should do

Although you had, I think, decided already not to give him that
piece of your mind.

After all, it wasn't as if he had done anything wrong.

Oh, that one, he said.

You have to imagine -

The boy was getting too big for ponies

So I bought him a horse

For two thousand pounds

Only for him to tell us, no more than about two weeks later,

That he had lost interest.

Why didn't you tell me that before I spent the two grand?

Was what I wanted to say.

Not that I cared about the money; that wasn't the important thing.

You have to imagine - I married late;

I was forty-nine when the boy was born

And he's just everything to me.

And the riding - well, the missus has always ridden

And the boy rode a pony

And we used to have these wonderful times

When they'd go out on the horses

And I'd walk behind with the dogs

And they'd turn around from time to time

And call out, 'Come on old man; try and keep up'

And it was bliss, you know, those wonderful happy family times

And then they just ended, just like that,

All on the whim of my nine-year-old son.

Now he seems to live in a world of his own.

But why did you want to hear all that again?

I put down my now-empty glass.

Shall we have one for the road? I asked.

He swirled the last inch in his glass and looked doubtful.

Do you think we should?

And then - Why not? he said.

DEAD SOULS/CHERRY BLOSSOM

10,000 souls on the cherry trees

10,000 true believers blossoming

10,000 mute magicians concealing nothing

The souls of jugglers without memories

Only the bird sounding wounded in love

Echoing the sorrow of the blossoms

How many springs can I have left?

Yet what a time to be alive

The blossoms do not think about their fall

The ripeness of their gorgeousness is all

HE SAID/SHE SAID

He said Let's do it in the park

We always do it in the dark

When I can hardly see

She said Oh, yes! That sounds a lark

To do it the public park

Where everyone can see

He said No absolutely not

I meant we'd find a hidden spot

Behind a bush or tree

She said But if we find that spot

And take off all that we have got

And someone comes to pee?

76

He said I didn't think that you'd

Object to doing something rude

You're always so broad-minded, free

She said You know I'm not a prude

But to be there in the nude

Upon my hands and knees

He got his way in the end of course

Behind a bush of prickly gorse

No-one came to look or pee

Only they were caught on CCTV

TOUTE DE TOUTE MES CHERIES

The owl of Minerva spreads her wings at the end of day

At dawn she folds herself in sleep

To whom can I complain?

From whom can I claim compensation?

Is it those bloody poets again,

Forever singing of love?

Or those philosophers:

"To love is to give what one does not have".

Gee, thanks for that advice; I suck it like a rusk

The owl of Minerva spreads her wings only at dusk

Remember the purple irises?

Their purple leaves wrapped tightly around their buds

Like a Paris dress around a woman's waist?

It would be too obvious to tell you how the newcomers razed

That garden, paved it for parking space;

But neither can I tell you, if I am honest,

That they were dreamt, and so, as I was, but a husk

The owl of Minerva spreads her wings only at dusk

Did you ever know that you had dreamt me?

Or did you forget the moment you awoke?

Imagine what that was like for me -

Nothing but a husk until you slept once more -

Except for the glimpse of the irises in May.

The owl of Minerva spreads her wings at the end of day

At dawn she folds herself in sleep.

EXTENDED FAMILY

I love them all to bits and pieces

All of them, not just Richard and the dog

But brothers, sisters, nephews, nieces,

Cousins, the next-door neighbours, Pam and Reg,

Which is why I keep them in the freezer,

Jointed, underneath the frozen veg.

LEARNING BY HEART

I thought she had gone forever

And that I could grieve and regret and feel sorry for myself

And make her departure the subject of poems

But she keeps coming back

Checking up on me

Honestly, she says - which is the way she always started

when she told me some home truths -

This place is a tip,

And she hoovers and fills the washing-machine and cuts my hair

I'm trying to work

I shout above the noise of the vacuum-cleaner

- Can't hear you, she trills, with a smirk

She *can* hear me; she's heard it all before,

The noise, the silence,

The sound of doors opening and closing

She has learned it all by heart

- For God's sake change the record, she used to cry.

I bet she doesn't say that to the vacuum-cleaner

Or the tumble-dryer

Even though they never change their tune

POEM IN A BOTTLE

I bottled up a poem

And launched it on the sea -

Fifteen years went by

And no-one rescued me.

I wrote verses about childhood -

How innocent and free -

But nobody was listening

From across the sea.

I wrote of love and marriage,

Of youth and beauty -

I waited by the shore

But nothing did I see.

I wrote of clouds and mountains,

Of flowers on the lea.

I listened for an echo

But no echo came to me.

I wrote of God and heaven,

Of how the world should be,

But when the waves came rolling in

They were empty.

I wrote of the dead and the dying,

Of a grave beneath a tree -

And I waited for an answer

From the silent sea.

I bottled up a poem

And sent it out to sea.

Sixteen years went by before

It washed back in to me.

FUNNY UNCLE

There's nothing especially funny about the word 'uncle'

Except that it makes a half-rhyme with the word 'funny',

And when Lear's Fool calls him 'nuncle'

It makes him, Lear, sound like the Fool.

But my Uncle Bill *was* a funny uncle.

He smoked a pipe and always slipped me money.

He never spoke of his wartime in the jungle,

Invited not hero-worship, but ridicule.

He never did anything after the war, my uncle.

I couldn't work out what he did for money.

He just had his pipe and his schoolboy chuckle,

Frittered his life away on a barstool.

He was funny because he wasn't a husband or father,

Only an uncle.

He'd been engaged but, after the war, he had no money,

That must have been the nub of it.

But he never complained about life being cruel.

And then, at the age of 80, in the care home

He fell in love, and she, Jo, also full of years,

Fell in love with him.

More of a funny uncle than ever then,

Except it wasn't funny, it was true and it was love.

"Funny, isn't it?" he told me while pouring the tea,

His eyes wet with something that wasn't tears,

"Getting married for the first time - a man of my years".

Jo held his hand and looked at him adoringly.

LOOKING BACK

Looking back, from halfway up the cliff

At the sea with glittering sunlight adorned

I say to myself it is as if

I have been granted a vision of glory,

And I stand, stock-still with awe

And ask, What more could you ever want than this?

And I answer -

More.

NOTES

The Judgement of Paris. Paris was the judge of a contest between the three most beautiful goddesses of Olympos - Aphrodite, Hera and Athena - for the prize of a golden apple. He chose Aphrodite, swayed by her promise to bestow upon him Helen, the most beautiful woman in the world, for his wife. It was his abduction of Helen that led to the Trojan War.

I Heard a Man on the Radio Say. The man I heard on the radio was the writer Colm Tóibín, who was the guest on *Desert Island Discs* on January 3, 2016. This is what he said: "Then of course you become a teenager... and I loved those melancholy songs, all about lost love. I didn't know anything about love! I didn't know anything about anything! But lost love seemed more real somehow than anything else you knew." The miserable love song he chose was Joni Mitchell's *The Last Time I Saw Richard.*

Yearning for Love. Patti Smith can be heard snarling, 'We don't need your fucking shit' on her account of The Who's *My Generation.*

It's an old idea, at least to me. The model is Horace's *Venus Be Merciful (Odes- Book IV, Ode I).* "Parce, precor, precor! Be merciful, I beg, I beg!" The words 'And now 'tis night. And now, he said, 'tis night' are taken from Elizabeth Barrett Browning's *Aurora Leigh.*

Does Your Restless Heart Mean I'm Still On Your Mind. There are many films and novels about private detectives aka PIs or gumshoes, but I've never come across a poem about one, so I thought I should write one. When reading this, you should imagine you're listening to an American radio show. There is even a commercial break!

Lascia la Spina. Leave the thorn, take the rose; you go searching for your pain. *Lascia la Spina* is an aria for soprano by Handel.

Toute de Toute Mes Cheries. Minerva, the Roman goddess of wisdom, is represented by an owl. According to the philosopher Hegel, the owl takes flight only when the shades of night are gathering. In other words, wisdom comes too late in the day. There is no point asking me what the title of this poem means - it came to me in a dream.

Anthony White is a spoken word poet. Born in London in 1954, for most of his working life he was a nurse. Now retired, he lives in Folkestone, where he writes and performs his work, mostly with Poets' Corner Folkestone, of which he is a founding member. He has also written and performed solo shows at Faversham Fringe Festival, and *Miserable Love Poetry* was the first of these (2018). Anthony has now revised this for publication and added a miscellany of other poems written between 2015 and 2021.

He claims to have invented the genre 'Miserable Love Poetry', but evidence suggests otherwise.

9 781739 881719